The Art of Moral Decision Making
Understanding the Psychology Behind Our Choices

Ambikey Mishra

ISBN xxx-x-xxxxx-xxx-x

Table of Contents

Introduction

The importance of moral decision-making

The importance of moral decision-making

Morality has been a subject of great interest and debate throughout human history. Philosophers, theologians, and psychologists have all grappled with the question of what constitutes right and wrong, and how individuals make moral decisions. In the present era, the study of morality has become increasingly interdisciplinary, with researchers from various fields contributing to our understanding of the psychological processes underlying moral decision-making. This article aims to provide an introduction to the complex interplay between morality and psychology, exploring the philosophical debates that have shaped our understanding of moral decision-making and the contemporary research that continues to inform this fascinating area of study.

In today's rapidly changing world, the process of moral decision-making has become increasingly complex and multifaceted. The present generation faces a unique set of challenges and opportunities, shaped by factors such as globalization, technological advancements, and shifting cultural norms. As a result, understanding the psychological processes that underlie moral decision-making has become more important than ever. This article aims to provide an introduction to the study of moral decision-making in the present generation, exploring the various factors that influence our ethical choices and the psychological mechanisms that guide our moral judgments.

The history of moral philosophy is rich and diverse, with thinkers from various cultures and time periods offering their insights into the nature of morality. From the ancient Greeks, such as Socrates, Plato, and Aristotle, to the Enlightenment philosophers, such as Immanuel Kant and Jeremy Bentham, the question of what constitutes moral behaviour has been a central concern. These philosophical debates have laid the groundwork for our understanding of morality, providing a foundation upon which contemporary psychologists can build.

One of the earliest and most influential theories of morality comes from the ancient Greek philosopher Plato. In his dialogues, Plato argued that moral behaviour is rooted in the pursuit of the highest good, which he identified as the "Form of the Good." According to Plato, individuals who have a clear understanding of this ultimate good will naturally act in morally virtuous ways. This idea has had a lasting impact on moral philosophy, with many subsequent thinkers building upon or critiquing Plato's conception of the good.

Another important figure in the history of moral philosophy is Immanuel Kant, who proposed a deontological approach to ethics. According to Kant, moral actions are determined by a set of universal moral principles, known as the "categorical imperative." This approach emphasizes the importance of duty and obligation in moral decision-making, asserting that individuals should act in accordance with these principles regardless of the consequences.

In contrast to Kant's deontological approach, utilitarianism, as proposed by Jeremy Bentham and later refined by John Stuart Mill, focuses on the consequences of actions. Utilitarianism posits that the morally right action is the one that produces the greatest overall happiness or pleasure for the greatest number of people. This consequentialist approach to morality has been influential in shaping modern ethical theories and has also informed psychological research on moral decision-making.

As the field of psychology has developed, researchers have increasingly turned their attention to the cognitive and emotional processes that underlie moral decision-making. One of the most influential theories in this area is Lawrence Kohlberg's theory of moral development, which posits that individuals progress through a series of stages as they develop their moral reasoning abilities. Kohlberg's work has been instrumental in shaping our understanding of how individuals make moral decisions and has inspired a wealth of research on the topic.

In recent years, the field of moral psychology has expanded to incorporate insights from neuroscience, evolutionary biology, and social psychology. Researchers have begun to explore the neural mechanisms that underlie moral decision-making, using techniques such as functional magnetic resonance imaging (fMRI) to investigate the brain regions involved in processing moral dilemmas. This research has revealed that moral decision-making is a complex process, involving both cognitive and emotional components.

Evolutionary perspectives on morality have also gained traction in recent years, with researchers examining the adaptive functions of moral behaviour. Some theories suggest that moral behaviour evolved as a means of promoting cooperation and social cohesion, while others argue that morality is a byproduct of other cognitive processes, such as the theory of mind and empathy.

Social psychology has also contributed to our understanding of moral decision-making, with researchers examining the role of situational factors and social influences on moral behaviour. This research has highlighted the importance of context in shaping moral decisions, demonstrating that individuals' moral judgments can be influenced by factors such as group dynamics, cultural norms, and authority figures. The study of morality and the psychology of decision-making is a rich and multifaceted field, with a long history of philosophical debate and a growing body of contemporary research. By examining the cognitive, emotional, and social processes that underlie moral decision-making, psychologists can gain valuable insights into the nature of human morality and the factors that shape our ethical choices.

The field of moral psychology has a rich history, with roots in both philosophy and psychology. Early philosophical theories of morality, such as those proposed by Plato, Aristotle, Kant, and Bentham, have laid the groundwork for our understanding of moral decision-making. These theories have been further developed and refined by contemporary psychologists, who have sought to uncover the cognitive, emotional, and social processes that underlie our moral judgments.

One of the key factors that influence moral decision-making in the present generation is the unprecedented access to information and diverse perspectives. The rise of the internet and social media has made it possible for individuals to engage with a wide range of ideas and viewpoints, which can both enrich and complicate the process of moral decision-making. This increased exposure to diverse perspectives can lead to a greater appreciation for the complexity of moral issues, as well as a heightened awareness of the potential consequences of our actions.

Another important factor shaping moral decision-making in the present generation is the growing emphasis on individualism and personal autonomy. As traditional sources of moral authority, such as religious institutions and cultural norms, have become less influential, individuals are increasingly encouraged to develop their own moral compass and make ethical decisions based on their personal values and beliefs. This shift towards individualism has both positive and negative implications for moral decision-making, as it can foster a greater sense of responsibility and self-reflection, but also lead to moral relativism and a lack of consensus on shared ethical principles.

The role of emotions in moral decision-making has also been a topic of growing interest among psychologists. Research has shown that emotions play a crucial role in shaping our moral judgments, with feelings such as empathy, guilt, and disgust influencing our perceptions of right and wrong. In the present generation, the role of emotions in moral decision-making may be particularly pronounced, as individuals are increasingly exposed to emotionally charged information and images through various media platforms. This emotional engagement can both enhance and hinder moral decision-making, as it can foster a greater sense of empathy and concern for others, but also lead to impulsive and biased judgments.

The influence of social and cultural factors on moral decision-making is another important area of study in moral psychology. Research has shown that our moral judgments are shaped by the social context in which we find ourselves, with factors such as group dynamics, cultural norms, and authority figures playing a significant role in guiding our ethical choices. In the present generation, the influence of social and cultural factors on moral decision-making may be particularly pronounced, as individuals navigate an increasingly diverse and interconnected world.

In addition to these external factors, the process of moral decision-making is also shaped by a range of cognitive processes and biases. Research has shown that individuals often rely on heuristics, or mental shortcuts when making moral judgments, which can lead to biased and inconsistent decisions. Furthermore, factors such as cognitive dissonance, confirmation bias, and fundamental attribution error can also influence our moral judgments, leading us to rationalize our actions and maintain a positive self-image.

In conclusion, the study of moral decision-making in the present generation is a complex and multifaceted endeavor, requiring an understanding of the various psychological, social, and cultural factors that shape our ethical choices. By examining the cognitive, emotional, and social processes that underlie moral decision-making, we can gain valuable insights into the nature of human morality and the factors that influence our ethical judgments. As we continue to explore this fascinating area of study, we can deepen our understanding of the challenges and opportunities faced by the present generation, and ultimately, contribute to the development of a more just and compassionate society.

CHAPTER 1

Theoretical Frameworks for Understanding Moral Decision-Making

Cognitive Developmental Theory

The cognitive-developmental theory was first proposed by Jean Piaget, a Swiss psychologist, in the 1920s. According to this theory, children go through distinct stages of cognitive development as they grow and mature. These stages are characterized by different ways of thinking, perceiving, and understanding the world around them.

Piaget identified four main stages of cognitive development: the sensorimotor stage, the pre-operational stage, the concrete operational stage, and the formal operational stage. Each stage is marked by specific cognitive abilities and limitations.

The sensorimotor stage, which lasts from birth to around two years of age, is characterized by the child's reliance on their senses and motor skills to explore and understand the world. During this stage, children develop object permanence, which is the understanding that objects continue to exist even when they are out of sight.

The pre-operational stage, which lasts from around two to seven years of age, is characterized by the child's increasing use of language and symbolic thinking. During this stage, children develop the ability to use symbols to represent objects and ideas, but they still struggle with logical reasoning and understanding the perspectives of others.

The concrete operational stage, which lasts from around seven to twelve years of age, is characterized by the child's increasing ability to think logically and understand cause-and-effect relationships. During this stage, children develop the ability to perform mental operations on concrete objects and ideas, but they still struggle with abstract thinking.

The formal operational stage, which begins around age twelve and continues into adulthood, is characterized by the individual's ability to think abstractly and reason logically about hypothetical situations. During this stage, individuals develop the ability to think critically and solve complex problems.

Piaget's cognitive-developmental theory has been influential in the field of psychology and has been used to inform educational practices and interventions. However, the theory has also been criticized for its emphasis on individual development and its lack of attention to social and cultural factors that may influence cognitive development.

In response to these criticisms, other theorists have proposed alternative models of cognitive development

    The Art of Moral Decision Making

that take into account the role of social and cultural factors. For example, Lev Vygotsky, a Russian psychologist, proposed the sociocultural theory of cognitive development, which emphasizes the role of social interaction and cultural context in shaping cognitive development.

According to Vygotsky, cognitive development is a collaborative process that occurs through social interaction and participation in cultural practices. Children learn from more knowledgeable others, such as parents, teachers, and peers, who provide guidance and support as they engage in challenging activities.

In conclusion, the cognitive-developmental theory is a prominent theory in the field of psychology that proposes that children go through distinct stages of cognitive development as they grow and mature. While the theory has been influential in informing educational practices and interventions, it has also been criticized for its emphasis on individual development and its lack of attention to social and cultural factors. Alternative models of cognitive development, such as the sociocultural theory, have been proposed to address these criticisms and provide a more comprehensive understanding of cognitive development.

Social Learning Theory

The social learning theory, as we have discussed earlier, emphasizes the role of observation, imitation, and modelling in shaping behaviour and personality. In the context of moral decision-making, this theory suggests that individuals learn moral values and principles through observation and modelling of the behaviour of others.

According to the social learning theory, moral decision-making is influenced by four main factors: attention, retention, reproduction, and motivation. Attention refers to the individual's ability to focus on and attend to the behaviour of others. Retention refers to the individual's ability to remember and store the observed behaviour in memory. Reproduction refers to the individual's ability to reproduce the observed behaviour. Motivation refers to the individual's desire or incentive to engage in the observed behaviour.

In the context of moral decision-making, attention is important because individuals must be able to recognize and attend to moral behaviour in order to learn from it. Retention is important because individuals must be able to remember and recall moral behaviour in order to apply it to their own

The Art of Moral Decision Making

decision-making. Reproduction is important because individuals must be able to reproduce moral behaviour in order to act in accordance with moral principles. Motivation is important because individuals must be motivated to engage in moral behaviour in order to act in accordance with moral principles.

Research has shown that social learning plays an important role in the development of moral decision-making. Children learn moral values and principles through observation and modelling of the behaviour of others, particularly parents, teachers, and peers. For example, children who observe their parents engaging in prosocial behaviour, such as helping others, are more likely to engage in prosocial behaviour themselves.

In addition to observation and modelling, social learning theory suggests that reinforcement and punishment also play a role in moral decision-making. Individuals are more likely to engage in moral behaviour if they receive positive reinforcement, such as praise or rewards, for their behaviour. Conversely, individuals are less likely to engage in moral behaviour if they receive negative reinforcement, such as criticism or punishment, for their behaviour.

Social learning theory also suggests that moral decision-making is influenced by social norms and expectations. Individuals are more likely to engage in moral behaviour if they perceive that it is expected or valued by their social group. Conversely, individuals are less likely to engage in moral behaviour if they perceive that it is not expected or valued by their social group. The social learning theory suggests that individuals learn moral values and principles through observation and modelling of the behaviour of others. Attention, retention, reproduction, and motivation are important factors in moral decision-making. Reinforcement and punishment, as well as social norms and expectations, also play a role in moral decision-making. Understanding the role of social learning in moral decision-making can help us to better understand how individuals develop moral values and principles, and how we can promote moral behaviour in ourselves and others.

Evolutionary Psychology

Evolutionary psychology is a theoretical approach to psychology that seeks to explain human behaviour and cognition in terms of evolutionary processes. According to this approach, human behaviour and cognition are shaped by natural selection, which favours traits and behaviours that enhance an individual's reproductive success. In the context of moral decision-making, evolutionary psychology suggests that moral values and principles have evolved as adaptations to the social and ecological challenges faced by our ancestors. These adaptations have been shaped by natural selection, which has favoured behaviours that promote cooperation, altruism, and social cohesion.

One of the key concepts in evolutionary psychology is inclusive fitness, which refers to the reproductive success of an individual and their close relatives. According to this concept, individuals are more likely to engage in behaviours that promote the survival and reproduction of themselves and their close relatives, as these behaviours increase their inclusive fitness. In the context of moral decision-making, inclusive fitness theory suggests that individuals are more likely to engage in behaviours that promote the survival and reproduction of their kin and social group. For example, individuals may be more likely to help a family member or friend in need, as this behaviour promotes the survival and reproduction of their kin and social group.

Another key concept in evolutionary psychology is the theory of reciprocal altruism, which suggests that individuals are more likely to engage in altruistic behaviour if they expect to receive benefits in return. According to this theory, individuals are more likely to help others if they expect to receive help in the future, as this behaviour promotes their own survival and reproduction. In the context of moral decision-making, reciprocal altruism theory suggests that individuals are more likely to engage in behaviours that promote the survival and reproduction of their social group if they expect to receive benefits in return. For example, individuals may be more likely to help a stranger in need if they expect that others will help them in the future, as this behaviour promotes the survival and reproduction of their social group.

Evolutionary psychology also suggests that moral decision-making is influenced by cognitive mechanisms that have evolved to solve specific adaptive problems. For example, the theory of kin selection suggests that

The Art of Moral Decision Making

individuals are more likely to help their close relatives, as this behaviour promotes their inclusive fitness. The theory of group selection suggests that individuals are more likely to engage in behaviours that promote the survival and reproduction of their social group, as this behaviour promotes their own survival and reproduction.

Evolutionary psychology suggests that moral values and principles have evolved as adaptations to the social and ecological challenges faced by our ancestors. Inclusive fitness theory and reciprocal altruism theory suggest that individuals are more likely to engage in behaviours that promote the survival and reproduction of themselves and their social group. Cognitive mechanisms that have evolved to solve specific adaptive problems also influence moral decision-making. Understanding the role of evolutionary psychology in moral decision-making can help us to better understand the origins and functions of moral values and principles, and how they have evolved to promote cooperation, altruism, and social cohesion.

CHAPTER 2

The Role of Emotions in Moral Decision-Making

The Nature of Moral Emotions Guilt, Shame, And Empathy

Moral emotions are powerful forces that shape our behaviour, influence our decisions, and guide our interactions with others. In this chapter, we will explore the nature of three fundamental moral emotions: guilt, shame, and empathy. These emotions play a crucial role in our moral development, moral decision-making, and social interactions. Without further ado, let us delve into the depths of these complex emotions.

Guilt

Guilt is a powerful and pervasive moral emotion. It arises when we believe we have violated a moral standard or committed a wrongdoing. This emotion can manifest in various ways, from a subtle nagging feeling to overwhelming remorse. Guilt serves as a moral compass, guiding our behaviour by helping us recognize when we've crossed ethical boundaries. It can push us to make amends, seek forgiveness, or take corrective actions. Guilt, in its healthy form, encourages self-reflection and personal growth, making it an essential emotion in our moral repertoire.

Shame

Shame is a closely related but distinct emotion from guilt. While guilt focuses on our actions, shame centers on our sense of self. When we experience shame, we believe we are inherently flawed, unworthy, or fundamentally bad due to our actions or attributes. Unlike guilt, which can motivate positive change, shame tends to be destructive. It erodes self-esteem and can lead to withdrawal, isolation, or even destructive behaviours. Understanding the difference between guilt and shame is vital for harnessing their moral guidance while avoiding the pitfalls of shame's harmful effects.

Empathy

Empathy is a foundational moral emotion, enabling us to connect with the experiences and emotions of others. It involves both cognitive and emotional components, allowing us to understand and share in someone else's perspective and feelings. Empathy plays a critical role in moral decision-making by helping us recognize the impact of our actions on others. It encourages compassion, altruism, and prosocial behaviour. Without empathy, our moral compass would be incomplete, as it anchors our moral judgments in the well-being of those around us.

The Complex Interplay

The interplay between guilt, shame, and empathy is intricate and dynamic. Guilt often arises from a heightened sense of empathy, as we become acutely aware of the pain or suffering we've caused others. Conversely, a lack of empathy can dull the experience of guilt, making it easier to justify harmful actions. Shame, on the other hand, can hinder empathy. When we feel deeply ashamed of ourselves, we may become too preoccupied with our own inadequacies to empathize effectively with others. This self-centered focus can undermine our ability to make moral decisions that prioritize the welfare of those around us.

Cultural Variations

Cultural factors significantly influence how guilt, shame, and empathy are perceived and experienced. In some cultures, guilt may be emphasized as a moral motivator, encouraging individuals to take responsibility for their actions. In contrast, shame might play a more prominent role in cultures where collective identity and social harmony are paramount. Empathy, too, can vary culturally. Some societies may prioritize empathy toward close-knit communities, while others extend it more broadly to encompass strangers and even animals. Understanding these cultural nuances is essential for a comprehensive exploration of moral emotions.

Developmental Aspects

The development of moral emotions begins in childhood and continues throughout our lives. Children often experience guilt and shame as they learn societal norms and values. As they grow, their capacity for empathy deepens, allowing them to navigate increasingly complex moral dilemmas. Parents, caregivers, and educators play pivotal roles in nurturing these moral emotions in children. They shape the way children perceive guilt, shame, and empathy, influencing their moral development and decision-making abilities as they mature into adults.

The Evolutionary Perspective

From an evolutionary standpoint, moral emotions like guilt, shame, and empathy have likely evolved as adaptive mechanisms for social living. They help maintain group cohesion and cooperation by discouraging harmful actions and encouraging prosocial behaviour. Guilt may have evolved as a signal to prevent social exclusion and promote cooperation within groups. Shame, while often maladaptive in excessive amounts, might have served as a mechanism to signal submission and conformity within social hierarchies. Empathy, meanwhile, facilitates cooperation and mutual support, reinforcing social bonds.

Coping with Moral Emotions

Effectively coping with moral emotions is essential for making sound moral decisions. Guilt can prompt positive change when we use it as a catalyst for personal growth and amends-making. To cope with shame, it's crucial to reframe it as a signal for self-improvement rather than a condemnation of our entire selves. Empathy, as a moral emotion, requires careful management. While it's vital for understanding others, excessive empathy can lead to emotional burnout and distress. Balancing empathy with self-care and boundaries is essential for maintaining our well-being while continuing to make compassionate choices.

Moral Emotions and Decision-Making

Guilt, shame, and empathy are not passive emotions; they actively shape our moral decision-making. Guilt can steer us away from harmful actions, prompting us to consider the consequences of our choices. Shame, when managed effectively, can motivate us to align our behaviour with our values. Empathy serves as the foundation for considering the well-being of others in our moral judgments.

However, these emotions are not infallible guides. Guilt can lead to excessive self-blame, inhibiting our ability to make objective decisions. Shame can paralyze us with self-doubt, preventing us from taking necessary actions. Empathy, if not balanced with rationality, may lead to biased judgments or decision fatigue.

Strategies for Harnessing Moral Emotions

To harness the power of moral emotions in our decision-making, we can employ several strategies:

1. **Self-awareness:** Cultivate self-awareness to recognize when guilt, shame, or empathy are influencing your decisions. Acknowledge these emotions without judgment.

2. **Self-compassion:** Treat yourself with the same compassion you would offer to others. Forgive yourself for past mistakes and view shame as an opportunity for growth.

3. **Perspective-taking:** Enhance your empathy by actively trying to see situations from others' viewpoints. This can help you make more compassionate and understanding decisions.

 The Art of Moral Decision Making

4. **Rationality:** Balance emotions with rational thinking. Consider the facts, consequences, and ethical principles alongside your emotional responses.

5. **Mindfulness:** Practice mindfulness techniques to stay present and manage overwhelming emotions effectively.

Moral emotions like guilt, shame, and empathy are the emotional threads woven into the fabric of our moral decision-making. Understanding their nature, complexities, and interplay is vital for becoming more conscious and ethical decision-makers.

These emotions, when harnessed effectively, guide us toward actions that align with our values and contribute to a more compassionate and just society. By recognizing their presence, acknowledging their influence, and employing strategies to navigate them, we can embark on a journey of moral growth and ethical decision-making.

The Impact of Emotions on Moral Decision-Making

Emotions are the heartbeat of our lives. They shape our experiences, color our perceptions, and play a pivotal role in our decision-making, especially in the moral domain. In this chapter, we delve deep into the intricate relationship between emotions and moral choices, exploring how various emotions, from empathy to anger, influence the decisions we make.

The Role of Empathy

Empathy, often regarded as the cornerstone of moral decision-making, is the ability to understand and share the feelings of others. When we empathize with someone, we step into their shoes, recognizing their pain, joy, or suffering. This emotional resonance guides our moral compass.

Empathy encourages us to consider the welfare and rights of others. It fosters compassion, altruism, and prosocial behaviour. When faced with a moral dilemma, empathy prompts us to ask, "How would I feel in their situation?" It fuels our drive to help those in need, making it a powerful force for ethical decision-making.

The Influence of Anger

Anger is a complex and potent emotion, often labeled as a negative force. However, in the realm of moral decision-making, anger can serve as a motivator for justice. When we witness an injustice or wrongdoing, anger can fuel our determination to right the wrong.

Anger can lead us to take action, to speak out against oppression, and to seek justice for ourselves and others. However, unchecked anger can also lead to impulsive and vengeful actions. Thus, understanding and harnessing anger's power is critical for making morally sound decisions.

The Weight of Guilt

Guilt is a moral emotion that arises when we believe we've violated a moral standard or caused harm to others. It serves as a moral compass, alerting us when we've crossed ethical boundaries. Guilt can influence our decisions in two distinct ways.

First, it can lead us to make amends and seek forgiveness. When we experience guilt, we may feel a compelling urge to rectify our actions and alleviate the suffering we've caused. This can drive us to engage in acts of kindness or restitution.

Second, guilt can also be paralyzing. Excessive guilt can lead to self-blame and a sense of unworthiness, inhibiting our ability to make rational and ethical decisions. Striking a balance between constructive guilt and debilitating self-blame is crucial for navigating the moral landscape effectively.

The Temptation of Fear

Fear, a primal and instinctive emotion, can significantly impact our moral decision-making. It often arises in situations where we perceive danger or potential harm. Fear can lead to self-preservation, prompting us to prioritize our safety over ethical considerations.

In moral dilemmas, fear can tempt us to make decisions that protect us from harm, even if those decisions compromise our values or the well-being of others. Recognizing the influence of fear on our choices is essential for making moral decisions that transcend self-preservation and prioritize ethical principles.

The Duality of Disgust

Disgust is a complex emotion that can influence moral judgments in contrasting ways. On one hand, it can serve as a protective mechanism, warning us against potential threats and contamination. In this context, disgust may help us make morally appropriate decisions by avoiding harmful or repugnant actions.

On the other hand, disgust can be a source of bias and prejudice. It can lead us to dehumanize others or stigmatize certain groups based on their appearance or behaviour. Recognizing the duality of disgust and its potential to influence our moral choices is essential for promoting fair and compassionate decision-making.

The Tug of Sympathy

Sympathy, often intertwined with empathy, involves feeling sorrow or pity for another person's suffering. While empathy encourages understanding, sympathy elicits a desire to alleviate another's pain. This emotion can be a powerful motivator for moral action.

When we feel sympathy, we may be driven to offer help, support, or comfort to those in need. Sympathy encourages us to prioritize the well-being of others, making it a force for ethical decision-making. However, like other emotions, it must be balanced with rationality to ensure that our actions are genuinely beneficial.

Navigating Moral Emotions

Understanding the impact of emotions on moral decision-making is essential, but it's equally crucial to navigate these emotions effectively. Here are some strategies for harnessing the power of emotions in ethical choices:

1. **Self-awareness:** Recognize when emotions are influencing your moral judgments. Cultivate mindfulness to pause and reflect on your emotional responses.

2. **Emotional regulation:** Develop skills to manage and balance your emotions, preventing them from clouding your judgment or leading to impulsive decisions.

3. **Empathy cultivation:** Practice empathy-building exercises to enhance your capacity to understand and connect with the experiences of others.

4. **Ethical principles:** Anchor your decisions in a strong ethical framework. Consider how your choices align with your values and principles, even when emotions run high.

5. **Reflective decision-making:** Take time to reflect on moral dilemmas, considering the perspectives of all involved parties and the long-term consequences of your choices.

    The Art of Moral Decision Making

Emotions are the threads that weave the fabric of our moral decision-making. From the profound influence of empathy to the motivating force of anger, emotions shape our ethical choices in profound ways.

Recognizing the impact of these emotions and learning to navigate them effectively is crucial for making morally sound decisions. By understanding the complex interplay between emotions and ethics, we can develop a more conscious and compassionate approach to moral decision-making, one that reflects our values and contributes to a more just and empathetic world.

The Role of Emotional Regulation in Moral Decision-Making

Emotions are a fundamental aspect of our humanity, influencing virtually every aspect of our lives, including the moral decisions we make. Yet, emotions are not uncontrollable forces that dictate our choices. Instead, we possess the capacity for emotional regulation, the ability to manage, modulate, and harness our emotions. In this chapter, we delve into the pivotal role of emotional regulation in the complex process of moral decision-making.

Emotional regulation refers to the conscious and unconscious strategies we use to modulate the intensity, duration, and expression of our emotions. It's the capacity to navigate the turbulent sea of feelings, guiding them in ways that align with our values, goals, and societal norms.

Effective emotional regulation is not about suppressing or denying emotions but rather about channeling them constructively. It involves recognizing and acknowledging our emotions, understanding their triggers, and choosing how to respond. Emotional regulation is a skill that can be cultivated and honed over time, making it a vital tool in the moral decision-making toolkit.

The Influence of Emotional Regulation

Emotional regulation plays a multifaceted role in the moral decision-making process. Here, we explore its impact from various angles:

1. **Impulse Control:** One of the key functions of emotional regulation is impulse control. Emotions like anger or fear can trigger impulsive actions that may not align with our ethical principles. Effective regulation allows us to pause, reflect, and choose a more considered response, even in emotionally charged situations.

2. **Ethical Consistency:** Emotional regulation helps maintain ethical consistency by preventing emotional hijacking. When we let strong emotions dictate our choices, we risk making decisions that are inconsistent with our values. Emotional regulation helps ensure that our actions are congruent with our moral principles.

3. **Compassionate Decision-Making:** Emotional regulation enables us to approach moral

dilemmas with compassion. By managing emotions like anger or disgust, we can better understand the perspectives of others and make decisions that prioritize their well-being.

4. **Conflict Resolution:** In situations of moral conflict, emotional regulation is essential for facilitating constructive dialogue and conflict resolution. It allows us to manage emotions that might otherwise escalate conflicts and hinder productive discussions.

Strategies for Effective Emotional Regulation

Developing emotional regulation skills is essential for making thoughtful and ethical decisions. Here are some strategies for enhancing emotional regulation in the context of moral decision-making:

1. **Mindfulness:** Mindfulness practices, such as meditation and deep breathing exercises, help increase self-awareness and emotional self-regulation. They enable us to observe our emotions without judgment and respond more deliberately.

2. **Cognitive Restructuring:** Challenge and reframe irrational or unhelpful thoughts that intensify negative emotions. By altering our

The Art of Moral Decision Making

thought patterns, we can change our emotional responses and make more rational decisions.

3. **Delayed Gratification:** Practice delaying immediate emotional reactions in favor of long-term goals and ethical considerations. This approach allows for more thoughtful responses to moral dilemmas.

4. **Self-compassion:** Treat yourself with kindness and understanding, especially when dealing with difficult emotions like guilt or shame. Self-compassion can prevent emotional overwhelm and facilitate better decision-making.

5. **Social Support:** Seek support and guidance from trusted friends, family, or professionals when facing complex moral decisions. Discussing your emotions and dilemmas with others can provide valuable perspectives and emotional relief.

6. **Emotional Intelligence:** Cultivate emotional intelligence by enhancing your ability to recognize and understand your own emotions and the emotions of others. This skill is invaluable for empathetic and ethical decision-making.

Emotional Regulation and Ethical Leadership

Emotional regulation is particularly crucial for ethical leadership. Leaders often face challenging moral decisions that can impact not only their own lives but also the lives of those they lead. Effective leaders must be adept at managing their emotions to make ethical choices and model ethical behaviour for others.

Ethical leaders use emotional regulation to:

1. **Foster a Positive Organizational Culture:** Leaders who regulate their emotions can create a positive and ethical organizational culture by managing conflicts, promoting open communication, and setting a tone of empathy and respect.

2. **Make Informed Decisions:** Emotional regulation enables leaders to make well-informed and ethical decisions, even in high-stakes situations. They avoid impulsive reactions that may harm their organization or its stakeholders.

3. **Build Trust:** Trust is foundational for leadership, and emotional regulation plays a crucial role in building and maintaining trust.

Leaders who manage their emotions effectively are perceived as more trustworthy and reliable.

4. **Resolve Ethical Dilemmas:** Ethical leaders often face complex dilemmas that require balancing conflicting values. Emotional regulation helps leaders navigate these dilemmas with fairness and integrity.

Emotional regulation is the lighthouse that guides our moral ship through the turbulent waters of life. In the realm of moral decision-making, it empowers us to steer clear of impulsive reactions and make choices that align with our values and principles.

As we explore the multifaceted impact of emotional regulation, we see that it is a skill of paramount importance. It underpins ethical consistency, compassion, and conflict resolution. It enables us to approach moral dilemmas with empathy and make decisions that consider the well-being of others.

Emotional regulation is a skill that can be developed and refined over time. Through mindfulness, cognitive restructuring, delayed gratification, and other strategies, we can become more adept at managing our emotions in the context of moral decision-making.

For leaders, in particular, emotional regulation is a cornerstone of ethical leadership. It shapes the culture of organizations, informs important decisions, builds trust, and empowers leaders to navigate complex ethical dilemmas.

In the end, emotional regulation is not a constraint on our emotions but a liberator of our ethical potential. It equips us to make moral decisions that reflect our values, contribute to a just and compassionate society, and ultimately define who we are as individuals and as leaders.

Chapter 3

The Influence of Social Norms on Moral Decision-making

The Impact of Social Norms on Moral Judgments

Social norms are the unwritten rules that govern our behaviour within a society or a group. These norms shape our interactions, influence our choices, and play a significant role in our moral judgments. In this chapter, we delve into the intricate relationship between social norms and moral judgments, exploring how societal expectations can both guide and sometimes challenge our ethical decisions.

The Power of Conformity

Human beings are inherently social creatures, and the desire to belong is a fundamental aspect of our nature. This drive for social acceptance often leads us to conform to the prevailing social norms within our communities. When we perceive that certain behaviours or values are widely accepted, we are more likely to align our own beliefs and actions with those norms.

Conformity to social norms can significantly impact our moral judgments. It can lead us to view actions that align with societal expectations as morally acceptable, even if they would be considered unethical in a different context. This influence can be subtle but pervasive, affecting our moral compass in various ways.

The Evolution of Norms

Social norms are not static; they evolve over time in response to changing societal values, beliefs, and circumstances. Norms can reflect cultural shifts, technological advances, or shifts in political and economic landscapes. As norms change, so too can our moral judgments.

For example, consider the evolving norms around environmental conservation. In the past, actions that were harmful to the environment might have been considered morally neutral or even virtuous. However, as awareness of ecological issues has grown, new social norms have emerged that prioritize sustainability and responsible stewardship of the planet. Consequently, behaviours that were once morally acceptable may now be viewed as unethical in the context of these evolving norms.

Cultural Variation

The impact of social norms on moral judgments varies across cultures. Different societies have distinct sets of norms, and what is considered morally acceptable in one culture may be seen as unethical in another. Cultural norms can influence how individuals perceive actions, values, and moral dilemmas.

For example, the concept of individualism versus collectivism plays a significant role in moral judgments. In cultures that prioritize individualism, personal autonomy and independence are highly valued. In contrast, collectivist cultures place greater emphasis on community, interdependence, and adherence to group norms. These cultural differences can lead to varying moral judgments in situations where individual rights and societal expectations collide.

Peer Influence

Our peers and social networks also exert a powerful influence on our moral judgments. People tend to seek approval and validation from their social groups, and this can impact their ethical decision-making. When our peers hold certain moral beliefs or values, we may be more likely to adopt those beliefs ourselves, even if they conflict with our personal convictions.

Peer pressure can lead individuals to conform to the moral norms of their social circle, even when those norms deviate from their own moral compass. This influence can be particularly strong among adolescents and young adults, who are navigating the complex terrain of identity formation and social belonging.

Social Norms and Ethical Dilemmas

In ethical dilemmas, the influence of social norms becomes particularly salient. These situations often present conflicting moral values or obligations, and individuals may turn to societal norms for guidance. However, relying solely on social norms can be problematic, as they may not always align with ethical principles.

Consider a scenario in which a social norm encourages discrimination against a particular group. Individuals who conform to this norm may justify their discriminatory actions as morally acceptable because they are following prevailing societal expectations. In such cases, an individual's moral judgment may be clouded by the influence of harmful norms.

Resisting Harmful Norms

Resisting harmful social norms is a significant ethical challenge. It requires individuals to have a strong moral compass, self-awareness, and the courage to stand up against the prevailing norms when they conflict with ethical principles.

To resist harmful norms effectively, individuals can:

1. **Cultivate Moral Autonomy:** Develop the ability to think critically and independently about moral issues, separate from the influence of social norms.

2. **Seek Diverse Perspectives:** Engage with a diverse range of viewpoints and perspectives to gain a more comprehensive understanding of moral dilemmas.

3. **Ethical Education**: Educate themselves about ethical theories and principles to make informed and ethically sound judgments.

4. **Practice Moral Courage:** Develop the courage to speak out against harmful norms, even when it is socially challenging or uncomfortable.

5. **Encourage Positive Change:** Advocate for positive changes in societal norms by engaging in constructive dialogue, activism, and awareness campaigns.

Social norms exert a significant influence on our moral judgments, shaping our perceptions of what is morally acceptable or unacceptable. The desire for social acceptance and conformity often leads individuals to align their moral beliefs and actions with prevailing norms.

However, it's essential to recognize that social norms are not inherently synonymous with ethical principles. Norms can evolve, vary across cultures, and even promote harmful behaviours. Therefore, individuals must cultivate moral autonomy, engage in critical thinking, and be willing to challenge harmful norms that conflict with their ethical convictions.

As we navigate the complex interplay between social norms and moral judgments, it becomes clear that ethics should not merely be a reflection of societal expectations. Instead, it should be guided by a deep commitment to universal principles of justice, compassion, and human dignity, even when those principles require us to challenge the status quo. In doing so, we contribute to a more just and ethical society that transcends the limitations of social norms.

The Role of Conformity in Moral Decision-making

Conformity is a powerful force that shapes our behaviour and influences the moral decisions we make. Human beings are social creatures, and the desire to fit in and belong to a group often leads us to conform to prevailing norms and expectations. In this chapter, we explore the complex interplay between conformity and moral decision-making, examining how the pressure to conform can both guide and challenge our ethical choices.

The Nature of Conformity

Conformity refers to the tendency to adjust one's thoughts, beliefs, and behaviours to align with the attitudes and behaviours of a group. It can manifest in various ways, from adopting fashion trends to adhering to societal norms and moral values. Conformity serves as a social glue that promotes cohesion and cooperation within communities.

In the context of moral decision-making, conformity plays a pivotal role in shaping our ethical judgments and actions. We often look to others to gauge what is morally acceptable, and our willingness to conform can influence the choices we make in morally ambiguous situations.

The Power of Social Norms

Social norms are unwritten rules that dictate appropriate behaviour within a society or group. They encompass a wide range of behaviours, from etiquette and dress codes to moral values and ethical principles. Social norms create a shared framework that helps individuals navigate complex social interactions and make decisions consistent with their group's expectations.

When confronted with moral dilemmas, individuals frequently turn to social norms for guidance. The pressure to conform to these norms can lead us to view actions that align with societal expectations as morally acceptable, even if they would be considered unethical in a different context. This influence can be subtle but pervasive, impacting our moral compass in various ways.

The Asch Conformity Experiment

One of the most famous experiments illustrating the power of conformity in moral decision-making is the Asch Conformity Experiment, conducted by Solomon Asch in the 1950s. In this study, participants were asked to compare the length of lines on different cards. However, all but one of the participants were confederates of the experimenter and purposely gave incorrect answers.

The results were striking. Even when the correct answer was obvious, many participants conformed to the group's incorrect responses. This demonstrated the profound influence that social pressure can have on individuals' willingness to deviate from their own judgment.

The Dual-Process Model

To understand how conformity impacts moral decision-making, we can turn to the dual-process model of social influence. This model distinguishes between two cognitive processes: automatic processing and controlled processing.

1. **Automatic Processing:** This is the intuitive, effortless mode of thinking where individuals may conform to social norms without much conscious thought. It often occurs when we rely on heuristics or "go with the flow" to fit in.

2. **Controlled Processing:** This mode involves deliberate, reflective thinking. Individuals engage in controlled processing when they

The Art of Moral Decision Making

critically evaluate the moral implications of a situation and make decisions based on reasoned judgment.

The interplay between these two processes can significantly affect moral decision-making. Automatic processing may lead to conformity with prevailing norms, while controlled processing can override this influence when individuals engage in ethical reflection.

Resisting Unethical Conformity

While conformity is a natural and often adaptive social behaviour, it can also lead to unethical outcomes. In some cases, group pressure may compel individuals to conform to behaviours that violate their own moral principles or ethical standards. Resisting unethical conformity requires a combination of self-awareness, moral courage, and critical thinking.

Strategies for resisting unethical conformity include:

1. **Self-reflection:** Encourage individuals to reflect on their personal values and ethical principles to strengthen their moral identity and resist pressures to conform to unethical behaviours.

2. **Group diversity:** Promote diversity within groups to encourage a wider range of

perspectives and reduce the likelihood of groupthink, where conformity to the group's view becomes unquestioned.

3. **Ethical leadership:** Ethical leaders can set an example by adhering to ethical principles and encouraging open dialogue about moral dilemmas within the group.

4. **Encouraging dissent:** Create an environment where dissenting opinions are valued and encouraged, fostering constructive discussion and ethical decision-making.

5. **Ethical training:** Provide education and training on ethical decision-making to enhance individuals' ability to resist unethical conformity.

Conformity is a powerful social force that influences our moral decisions by shaping our perceptions of what is morally acceptable or unacceptable. The desire to belong to a group often leads us to conform to prevailing social norms and expectations, which can guide our ethical choices in both positive and negative ways.

While conformity serves as a social glue that promotes cooperation and cohesion within communities, it can

The Art of Moral Decision Making

also lead to unethical outcomes when individuals succumb to group pressure that conflicts with their own moral principles. Recognizing the impact of conformity on moral decision-making is essential for individuals and organizations striving to make ethical choices that align with their values and principles.

Resisting unethical conformity requires self-awareness, moral courage, and critical thinking. By fostering environments that encourage diverse perspectives, dissenting opinions, and ethical leadership, we can mitigate the negative influence of conformity and promote ethical decision-making that transcends the limitations of group pressure. Ultimately, ethical choices should be guided by a deep commitment to universal principles of justice, compassion, and human dignity, even in the face of social pressures to conform.

The Impact of Group Dynamics on Moral Decision-Making

Human beings are inherently social creatures, and our moral decision-making is often influenced by the dynamics of the groups we belong to. Group dynamics encompass the complex interactions, norms, roles, and hierarchies that shape how individuals within a group behave and make decisions. In this chapter, we explore the profound impact of group dynamics on moral decision-making, examining how group influence can both enhance and challenge our ethical choices.

The Power of Group Influence

Group dynamics have a profound impact on our moral judgments and actions. When individuals belong to a group, they are influenced by various factors, including conformity, peer pressure, shared norms, and the desire to maintain group cohesion. These factors can guide individuals' moral decisions in both positive and negative ways.

Positive Aspects of Group Dynamics

1. **Support and Encouragement:** Groups can provide emotional support and encouragement for individuals to make ethical choices.

Knowing that others share their values can bolster individuals' confidence in their moral judgments.

2. **Collaboration:** Group dynamics can facilitate collaboration and collective decision-making that leads to morally sound outcomes. Groups can pool diverse perspectives and knowledge to arrive at more thoughtful ethical judgments.

3. **Accountability:** The presence of others in a group can promote accountability for one's actions. Individuals may be more inclined to make ethical decisions when they know they will be held responsible by their peers.

Negative Aspects of Group Dynamics

1. **Conformity:** The pressure to conform to the norms and values of a group can lead individuals to make unethical decisions that align with the group's expectations, even when those decisions conflict with their personal moral compass.

2. **Groupthink:** Groupthink is a phenomenon in which group members prioritize consensus and harmony over critical thinking and ethical

decision-making. It can result in flawed moral judgments and unethical actions.

3. **Diffusion of Responsibility:** In larger groups, individuals may feel a reduced sense of personal responsibility for their actions, leading to moral complacency and a willingness to engage in unethical behaviour.

Role of Leadership

Leaders within a group play a pivotal role in shaping group dynamics and influencing moral decision-making. Ethical leaders can set an example by adhering to ethical principles, fostering open dialogue about moral dilemmas, and promoting ethical norms within the group.

Conversely, leaders who condone or engage in unethical behaviour can create a culture of moral permissiveness within the group. Such leaders can influence members to prioritize loyalty to the leader over ethical considerations, leading to a breakdown in moral decision-making.

The Bystander Effect

The bystander effect is a psychological phenomenon in which individuals are less likely to offer help or intervene in an emergency situation when others are present. This effect is closely tied to group dynamics and can impact moral decision-making in situations where intervention is required to prevent harm.

In moral dilemmas where bystanders witness unethical behaviour within a group, the presence of others can lead to diffusion of responsibility. Individuals may refrain from intervening because they assume that someone else will step in or because they fear social repercussions for challenging the group's actions.

The Role of Group Identity

Group identity, the sense of belonging to a particular group, strongly influences moral decision-making. Individuals often prioritize the values and norms of their group over external ethical principles. This in-group favoritism can lead to biased moral judgments, where individuals perceive actions by members of their group as more morally acceptable than similar actions by outsiders.

Group identity can also lead to out-group derogation, where individuals view members of other groups as less moral or less deserving of ethical considerations. This bias can contribute to intergroup conflicts and ethical challenges.

Resisting Negative Group Dynamics

Resisting negative group dynamics and making ethical decisions within a group setting can be challenging but essential. Here are strategies for promoting ethical decision-making in groups:

1. **Ethical Leadership:** Encourage ethical leadership within the group to set a positive example, foster open discussions about moral dilemmas, and promote ethical norms.

2. **Group Diversity:** Diverse groups with a range of perspectives can mitigate groupthink and encourage more comprehensive ethical decision-making.

3. **Ethical Education:** Provide education and training on ethical decision-making to enhance group members' ability to recognize and address moral dilemmas.

4. **Encourage Dissent:** Create an environment where dissenting opinions are valued and encouraged, allowing for constructive discussions about ethical choices.

5. **Shared Values:** Develop a strong sense of shared values and ethical principles within the group to guide decision-making.

Group dynamics exert a profound influence on moral decision-making, shaping how individuals within a group perceive, judge, and respond to ethical dilemmas. These dynamics can either enhance or challenge ethical choices, depending on various factors such as conformity, leadership, group identity, and the presence of bystanders.

While group dynamics can promote ethical behaviour through support, collaboration, and accountability, they can also lead to unethical actions through conformity, groupthink, and diffusion of responsibility. Recognizing the impact of group dynamics is essential for individuals and organizations striving to make ethical decisions that align with their values and principles.

Resisting negative group dynamics requires a combination of ethical leadership, diversity, education, and an environment that encourages dissent. By fostering ethical decision-making within groups, we can navigate the complex interplay of social influences and uphold universal principles of justice, compassion, and human dignity. Ultimately, ethical choices should transcend the limitations of group dynamics, ensuring that moral decisions prioritize the welfare of individuals and society as a whole.

Chapter 4

The Impact of Personal Values on Moral Decision-making

The Nature of Personal Values

Moral decision-making is a complex and deeply personal process, influenced by a myriad of factors. At the core of this intricate web of influences lie personal values. Personal values are the fundamental beliefs and principles that shape an individual's understanding of right and wrong, good and bad, and guide their ethical compass. In this chapter, we delve into the profound impact of personal values on the moral decisions we make, examining the nature of these values and how they interact to guide our choices.

Understanding Personal Values

Personal values, often acquired through upbringing, culture, and life experiences, serve as the building blocks of our moral framework. They are not merely abstract ideals; they are deeply ingrained beliefs that shape our perceptions and attitudes. These values encompass a wide spectrum of principles, ranging from honesty and empathy to justice and integrity. They are the inner compass that helps us navigate the complex terrain of moral dilemmas.

The Nature of Personal Values

Personal values are not static entities but dynamic and evolving aspects of an individual's identity. They are shaped by various factors, including culture, family, religion, and personal experiences. Understanding the nature of personal values is crucial in comprehending their impact on moral decision-making.

One key aspect of personal values is their hierarchy. Individuals prioritize certain values over others, creating a unique value system. For example, someone may value honesty above all else and be willing to make personal sacrifices to uphold it. Conversely, another individual might prioritize loyalty or family unity as their highest values, which could lead to different moral choices in specific situations.

The Influence of Personal Values on Moral Decision-making

1. **Conflict Resolution:** Personal values often collide in moral dilemmas. Consider a scenario where honesty conflicts with loyalty. If honesty is paramount to an individual, they may choose to reveal a friend's wrongdoing despite the potential harm to the friendship. In contrast, someone who values loyalty more might keep the wrongdoing a secret to preserve the relationship. The prioritization of values profoundly impacts the outcome of moral decisions.

   The Art of Moral Decision Making

2. **Social and Cultural Factors:** Personal values are not developed in a vacuum. Society and culture play a significant role in shaping these values. For instance, in cultures that prioritize collectivism, values like community and harmony may take precedence over individualism and autonomy. As a result, moral decisions may align more with community interests than personal ones.

3. **Emotional Impact:** Emotions often intertwine with personal values in moral decision-making. A person who highly values empathy may be more prone to feel deep emotional distress when faced with a moral dilemma involving harm to others. These emotions can influence the decision-making process, sometimes leading to choices driven by compassion or guilt.

4. **Developmental Stages:** Personal values evolve as individuals progress through various life stages. What one values in adolescence may differ significantly from what they prioritize in adulthood. This evolution can lead to shifts in moral decision-making. For instance, the pursuit of personal success might be a dominant

value in early adulthood, but as one matures, values like family and community may take precedence.

5. **Cognitive Processes:** Cognitive biases and reasoning also play a role in how personal values affect moral decisions. Confirmation bias, for example, can lead individuals to interpret situations in a way that aligns with their preexisting values. This can reinforce their moral choices based on those values.

Cultivating Ethical Decision-making

Understanding the intricate relationship between personal values and moral decision-making can be instrumental in cultivating ethical decision-making skills. Here are some strategies:

1. **Self-Reflection:** Regularly assess and reflect on your personal values. Consider how they align with your moral choices and whether they are evolving over time.

2. **Critical Thinking:** Be aware of cognitive biases and engage in critical thinking when faced with moral dilemmas. Evaluate the situation objectively rather than solely relying on your values.

                    The Art of Moral Decision Making

3. **Seek Diverse Perspectives:** Encourage dialogue with individuals who hold different values. Exposure to diverse viewpoints can broaden your perspective and enhance your ability to empathize with alternative moral choices.

4. **Ethical Education:** Invest in ethical education and discussions. Books, courses, and discussions on ethics can provide valuable insights and tools for making morally sound decisions.

5. **Mentorship:** Seek guidance from mentors or role models who demonstrate ethical decision-making aligned with your values.

Personal values are the foundational pillars of moral decision-making. They are not static but evolve over time, influenced by numerous factors. The interplay between personal values and moral choices is intricate, often leading to challenging dilemmas. However, by understanding the nature of personal values and their profound impact on decision-making, individuals can navigate moral complexities with greater clarity and integrity, contributing to a more ethical and compassionate society.

The Impact of Conflicting Values on Moral Decision-Making

Moral decision-making is a complex and deeply personal process that reflects our ethical principles and values. However, this process becomes particularly challenging when conflicting values come into play. In this chapter, we will explore the intricate impact of conflicting values on the moral decision-making process. We will examine the nature of these conflicts, their emotional toll, and strategies to navigate them effectively.

Understanding Conflicting Values

Values are the moral compasses that guide our actions, and they are rarely monolithic. Each individual possesses a unique set of values, formed through life experiences, upbringing, and cultural influences. These values are not static but form a dynamic network that can lead to conflicts when they clash in specific situations.

Conflicting values occur when two or more of these deeply held principles collide, creating moral dilemmas that challenge our ethical resolve. It's essential to understand that these conflicts are not a sign of inconsistency but rather a testament to the complexity of human values.

The Nature of Conflicting Values

To comprehend the impact of conflicting values on moral decision-making, it is crucial to grasp their nature:

1. **Value Hierarchy:** Values are not equal in significance; individuals prioritize certain values over others. This hierarchical structure influences the choices we make. For instance, an individual who values truth above all else may find it difficult to withhold information even in situations where loyalty is at stake.

2. **Contextual Dependence:** Conflicting values often depend on the specific context of a moral dilemma. What may seem like a straightforward decision in one context can become a complex issue when conflicting values are considered. This contextual dependence adds layers of complexity to moral decision-making.

3. **Emotional Turmoil:** Conflicting values frequently evoke strong emotions. Guilt, anxiety, and inner turmoil are common emotional responses when individuals grapple

with moral dilemmas. These emotions can cloud judgment and add to the complexity of decision-making.

The Impact of Conflicting Values on Moral Decision-Making

1. **Moral Dilemmas:** Conflicting values are at the heart of moral dilemmas. These dilemmas arise when individuals must choose between two or more morally significant options, each with its own ethical merits and drawbacks. The absence of a clear-cut right or wrong answer can be distressing.

2. **Stress and Anxiety:** The emotional turmoil triggered by conflicting values often leads to stress and anxiety. Individuals may be tormented by self-doubt, fearing that they will make the wrong choice, especially when the stakes are high.

3. **Decision Paralysis:** In some instances, conflicting values can lead to decision paralysis. When individuals are unable to resolve the internal conflict, they may become immobilized and unable to make any decision, which can itself have moral consequences.

 The Art of Moral Decision Making

4. **Compromise and Resolution:** Conflicting values can also lead to creative solutions and compromises. For example, an individual facing a conflict between honesty and loyalty may choose to be honest while carefully considering how to minimize harm to the trust of a friend.

Navigating Conflicting Values

While conflicting values can be challenging, individuals can develop strategies to navigate these moral dilemmas effectively:

1. **Self-Reflection:** Begin by reflecting on your values and their hierarchy. Understanding which values hold the most weight in different contexts can provide clarity when conflicts arise.

2. **Consider Consequences:** Carefully evaluate the potential consequences of each choice when values clash. Analyze the short-term and long-term impacts of your decisions on yourself and others.

3. **Seek Input:** Consult with trusted friends, mentors, or professionals when facing difficult moral dilemmas. They can offer alternative

perspectives and insights that may help you make a more informed choice.

4. **Ethical Frameworks:** Familiarize yourself with various ethical frameworks, such as utilitarianism, deontology, and virtue ethics. These frameworks can provide guidance and structure when navigating conflicting values.

5. **Mindfulness and Emotional Regulation:** Practice mindfulness techniques and emotional regulation to manage the emotional distress that can accompany conflicting values. Techniques like meditation and deep breathing can help in making decisions more calmly.

Conflicting values are an intrinsic part of the human experience, and they have a profound impact on moral decision-making. These conflicts can create moral dilemmas that are emotionally challenging and often lack clear-cut solutions. However, by understanding the nature of conflicting values, recognizing their emotional effects, and employing thoughtful strategies, individuals can navigate these dilemmas with greater clarity and integrity.

Conflicting values serve as a reminder of the complexity of moral decision-making. They illustrate

 The Art of Moral Decision Making

that ethical choices are rarely straightforward but often exist in shades of gray. Embracing this complexity and approaching moral dilemmas with empathy and thoughtfulness can lead to more ethical and compassionate outcomes.

Chapter 5

The Role of Cognitive Biases and Heuristics in Moral Decision-Making

The Nature of Cognitive Biases and Heuristics

Moral decision-making is a complex and intricate process that involves evaluating actions and choices based on ethical principles and values. However, this process is not immune to the influence of cognitive biases and heuristics, which can shape our moral judgments and decisions. In this chapter, we delve into the nature of these cognitive shortcuts, explore how they impact moral decision-making, and consider strategies to mitigate their effects.

Understanding Cognitive Biases and Heuristics

Cognitive biases and heuristics are cognitive shortcuts that our brains use to simplify complex information processing. While they often serve us well in everyday decision-making, they can lead to systematic errors in judgment, especially in morally charged situations.

1. **Cognitive Biases:** These are systematic patterns of deviation from norm or rationality in judgment, often occurring due to mental shortcuts. Cognitive biases can influence our perceptions, interpretations, and decision-

making processes. In the context of moral decisions, several biases come into play.

2. **Heuristics:** Heuristics are mental shortcuts or "rules of thumb" that help us make quick decisions with minimal cognitive effort. They can be helpful in simplifying complex problems but may lead to errors in judgment when applied inappropriately.

Cognitive Biases and Heuristics in Moral Decision-Making

1. **Confirmation Bias:** Confirmation bias is the tendency to seek, interpret, and remember information in a way that confirms our preexisting beliefs or values. In moral decision-making, this bias can lead us to selectively focus on information that supports our initial judgments, reinforcing our existing moral views and potentially ignoring relevant facts.

2. **Moral Luck Bias:** This bias involves attributing moral judgments to factors beyond an individual's control, such as luck or circumstances. For example, someone may perceive a successful person as morally upright due to their success, even if their actions are

The Art of Moral Decision Making

ethically questionable. Conversely, a person who faces adversity may be unfairly judged as morally deficient.

3. **Fundamental Attribution Error:** The fundamental attribution error is the tendency to attribute the behaviour of others to internal characteristics (e.g., personality traits) while attributing our own behaviour to external factors (e.g., situational circumstances). In moral judgments, this can lead to unfair assessments of others' character while giving ourselves leniency for similar actions.

4. **The Dunning-Kruger Effect:** This cognitive bias refers to the tendency of individuals with low ability in a particular area to overestimate their competence and knowledge in that domain. In moral decision-making, this bias can lead people to make judgments without fully understanding the complexity of the moral dilemma, resulting in misguided decisions.

5. **Availability Heuristic:** The availability heuristic is the tendency to rely on readily available information or examples that come to mind when making judgments. In moral decision-making, this can lead to biased

judgments based on the prominence of certain moral issues in the media or recent events, rather than a comprehensive evaluation of the situation.

The Impact of Cognitive Biases and Heuristics on Moral Decision-Making Cognitive biases and heuristics can significantly impact moral decision-making in several ways:

1. **Hasty Judgments:** Heuristics can lead to quick, often hasty, moral judgments. Instead of carefully considering the nuances of a moral dilemma, individuals may rely on readily available heuristics, leading to biased or oversimplified decisions.

2. **Unfair Assessments:** Cognitive biases, such as the fundamental attribution error, can result in unfair assessments of others' character and motivations. This can lead to moral judgments that are overly harsh or lenient, depending on the bias at play.

3. **Resistance to Change:** Confirmation bias can make individuals resistant to changing their moral views, even when presented with compelling evidence that contradicts their

 The Art of Moral Decision Making

beliefs. This resistance to new information can hinder moral growth and development.

4. **Inconsistent Judgments:** The influence of cognitive biases can lead to inconsistent moral judgments. People may make different moral assessments of similar situations based on factors such as timing, context, or the framing of the dilemma.

Mitigating the Impact of Cognitive Biases and Heuristics

While cognitive biases and heuristics are natural aspects of human cognition, there are strategies to mitigate their impact on moral decision-making:

1 **Awareness:** The first step in combating cognitive biases and heuristics is awareness. Recognize that these shortcuts exist and can influence your moral judgments. Being mindful of their potential impact is essential for making more informed decisions.

2. **Critical Thinking:** Encourage critical thinking when faced with moral dilemmas. Question your initial judgments and consider alternative viewpoints. Seek out information from diverse sources to reduce confirmation bias.

3. **Reflective Decision-Making:** Take time to reflect on moral decisions rather than relying on quick, heuristic-based judgments. Give yourself the opportunity to consider the complexities of the situation and its ethical implications.

4. **Consultation:** Seek input and advice from trusted individuals or experts when facing complex moral dilemmas. Consulting others can provide valuable perspectives that may counteract the influence of biases.

5. **Education and Training:** Invest in ethical education and training. Learning about different ethical frameworks and engaging in discussions about moral issues can help individuals develop a more nuanced and informed approach to moral decision-making.

Cognitive biases and heuristics are inherent aspects of human cognition that can impact our moral decision-making. They can lead to hasty judgments, unfair assessments, and resistance to change in our moral views. However, with awareness, critical thinking, and a commitment to reflective decision-making, individuals can mitigate the influence of these cognitive shortcuts and make more informed and ethical choices.

Recognizing the nature of cognitive biases and heuristics in moral decision-making is a crucial step toward developing a more thoughtful and empathetic approach to ethical dilemmas. While they may never be fully eliminated, their effects can be minimized, allowing individuals to navigate complex moral terrain with greater clarity and integrity.

The Impact of Cognitive Biases and Heuristics on Moral Reasoning

Moral reasoning is a complex cognitive process that involves evaluating actions and decisions based on ethical principles and values. However, this process is not immune to the influence of cognitive biases and heuristics, which can shape our moral judgments and reasoning. In this chapter, we will explore the profound impact of these cognitive shortcuts on moral reasoning, how they affect our ethical decisions, and strategies to enhance moral reasoning in the face of such biases.

Cognitive Biases and Heuristics in Moral Reasoning

1. **Confirmation Bias:** Confirmation bias is the tendency to seek, interpret, and remember information that confirms our preexisting beliefs or values. In moral reasoning, this bias can lead us to selectively focus on information that supports our initial moral judgment, reinforcing our existing ethical views while neglecting contrary evidence.

2. **Moral Luck Bias:** This bias involves attributing moral judgments to factors

The Art of Moral Decision Making

beyond an individual's control, such as luck or circumstances. For example, someone may perceive a successful person as morally upright due to their success, even if their actions are ethically questionable. Conversely, a person facing adversity may be unfairly judged as morally deficient.

3. **Fundamental Attribution Error:** The fundamental attribution error is the tendency to attribute the behaviour of others to internal characteristics (e.g., personality traits) while attributing our own behaviour to external factors (e.g., situational circumstances). In moral reasoning, this bias can lead to unfair assessments of others' character and motivations.

4. **The Dunning-Kruger Effect:** This cognitive bias refers to the tendency of individuals with low competence in a particular area to overestimate their knowledge and competence in that domain. In moral reasoning, this bias can lead people to make judgments without fully understanding the complexity of moral dilemmas, resulting in misguided ethical decisions.

5. **Availability Heuristic:** The availability heuristic is the tendency to rely on readily available information or examples that come to mind when making judgments. In moral reasoning, this can lead to biased judgments based on the prominence of certain moral issues in the media or recent events, rather than a comprehensive evaluation of the situation.

The Impact of Cognitive Biases and Heuristics on Moral Reasoning

Cognitive biases and heuristics can significantly impact moral reasoning in several ways:

1. **Simplified Reasoning:** Heuristics can lead to simplified moral reasoning, reducing complex ethical dilemmas to quick, often hasty judgments. Instead of considering the intricacies of a moral dilemma, individuals may rely on readily available heuristics, which can result in biased or superficial moral reasoning.

2. **Biased Assessments:** Cognitive biases, such as the fundamental attribution error, can result in biased assessments of others' character and motivations. This can lead to moral reasoning

 The Art of Moral Decision Making

that is overly harsh or lenient, depending on the bias at play.

3. **Resistance to Change:** Confirmation bias can make individuals resistant to changing their moral views, even when presented with compelling evidence that contradicts their beliefs. This resistance to new information can hinder moral growth and development.

4. **Inconsistent Reasoning:** The influence of cognitive biases can lead to inconsistent moral reasoning. People may apply different moral standards to similar situations based on factors such as timing, context, or the framing of the dilemma.

Enhancing Moral Reasoning in the Face of Cognitive Biases and Heuristics. While cognitive biases and heuristics are natural aspects of human cognition, there are strategies to enhance moral reasoning and mitigate their impact:

1. **Awareness:** The first step in combating cognitive biases and heuristics is awareness. Recognize that these shortcuts exist and can influence your moral reasoning. Being mindful

of their potential impact is essential for making more informed moral decisions.

2. **Critical Thinking:** Encourage critical thinking when faced with moral dilemmas. Question your initial judgments and consider alternative viewpoints. Seek out information from diverse sources to reduce confirmation bias.

3. **Reflective Reasoning:** Take time to engage in reflective moral reasoning rather than relying solely on quick, heuristic-based judgments. Give yourself the opportunity to consider the complexities of the situation and its ethical implications.

4. **Consultation:** Seek input and advice from trusted individuals or experts when facing complex moral dilemmas. Consulting others can provide valuable perspectives that may counteract the influence of biases.

5. **Ethical Education:** Invest in ethical education and training. Learning about different ethical frameworks and engaging in discussions about moral issues can help individuals develop a more nuanced and informed approach to moral reasoning.

　　　　　The Art of Moral Decision Making

Cognitive biases and heuristics are integral components of human cognition that can impact our moral reasoning. They can lead to simplified reasoning, biased assessments, resistance to change, and inconsistent ethical judgments. However, with awareness, critical thinking, and a commitment to reflective moral reasoning, individuals can mitigate the influence of these cognitive shortcuts and make more informed and ethical decisions.

Recognizing the nature of cognitive biases and heuristics in moral reasoning is a crucial step toward developing a more thoughtful and empathetic approach to ethical dilemmas. While they may never be completely eliminated, their effects can be minimized, allowing individuals to engage in moral reasoning with greater clarity and integrity.

Strategies for Overcoming Cognitive Biases and Heuristics in Moral Decision-making

Moral decision-making is a complex cognitive process that can be influenced by cognitive biases and heuristics, leading to errors in judgment and ethical reasoning. However, individuals can develop strategies to overcome these cognitive shortcuts and make more informed and ethically sound decisions. In this chapter, we explore effective strategies for mitigating the impact of cognitive biases and heuristics in the realm of moral decision-making.

Recognizing Cognitive Biases and Heuristics

Before delving into strategies for overcoming cognitive biases and heuristics, it is essential to recognize when these mental shortcuts may be at play in moral decision-making. Some signs that biases and heuristics may be influencing your judgments include:

1. **Rapid Decision-Making:** When you find yourself making quick and emotionally driven moral judgments without considering all relevant information.

2. **Selective Information Processing:** If you tend to seek out and pay more attention to information

that confirms your preexisting beliefs or values while dismissing contradictory evidence.

3. **Inconsistent Moral Judgments:** When you apply different moral standards to similar situations or make moral judgments that vary based on timing, context, or framing.

4. **Emotional Reactivity:** If you experience strong emotional reactions, such as anger, fear, or guilt, when faced with moral dilemmas, these emotions may be influencing your judgments.

Strategies for Overcoming Cognitive Biases and Heuristics

1. **Awareness and Mindfulness:**

   - *Practice Self-Awareness:* Cultivate self-awareness regarding your own cognitive biases and heuristics. Acknowledge that everyone is susceptible to these mental shortcuts, including yourself.

   - *Mindfulness Meditation:* Engage in mindfulness meditation to develop the ability to observe your thoughts and emotions without immediate judgment. This can help you recognize when cognitive biases are influencing your moral reasoning.

2. **Seek Diverse Perspectives:**

   – *Diverse Input:* Actively seek out diverse perspectives and opinions when facing moral dilemmas. Engaging with individuals who hold different values and beliefs can help you gain a broader understanding of the ethical implications of a situation.

   – *Devil's Advocate:* Encourage critical thinking by adopting the role of a "devil's advocate" when analyzing moral dilemmas. Challenge your initial judgments by considering alternative viewpoints.

3. **Slow Down and Reflect:**

   – *Reflective Reasoning:* Take your time to engage in reflective moral reasoning. Avoid making snap judgments and allow yourself the opportunity to think deeply about the complexities of the moral dilemma.

   – *Temporal Perspective:* Consider how your moral judgments may evolve over time. Imagine looking back on your decision from the future and assess whether it aligns with your long-term values and principles.

4. **Utilize Ethical Frameworks:**

   – *Familiarize Yourself:* Learn about various ethical frameworks, such as utilitarianism, deontology, virtue ethics, and others.

Understanding these frameworks can provide structured guidance in moral decision-making.

- *Apply Ethical Principles:* Apply the principles of ethical frameworks to analyze moral dilemmas systematically. Evaluate the consequences, duties, and virtues involved in a decision to arrive at a well-reasoned judgment.

5. Consult Trusted Advisors:

- *Seek Expert Guidance:* Consult with trusted mentors, friends, or professionals who possess expertise in ethics or the specific domain relevant to the moral dilemma. Their insights can offer valuable guidance.

- *Peer Discussions:* Engage in open and respectful discussions with peers about moral issues. Peer input can provide diverse perspectives and help you refine your moral reasoning.

6. Consider Consequences:

- *Consequential Analysis:* Assess the potential consequences of your moral decisions on various stakeholders, including yourself and others. Consider short-term and long-term outcomes and the overall impact on well-being and justice.

- *Hypothetical Testing:* Imagine hypothetical scenarios that explore the different outcomes of your moral decisions. This thought experiment can help you anticipate the consequences of your choices.

7. **Ethical Education and Training:**

   - *Continuous Learning:* Invest in ethical education and training. Attend workshops, seminars, or courses focused on ethics and moral reasoning to develop your skills further.

   - *Case Studies:* Study real-life ethical case studies to gain insights into how individuals and organizations have navigated complex moral dilemmas. Analyze these cases critically to refine your moral reasoning abilities.

8. **Ethical Decision-Making Models:**

   - *Use Decision-Making Models:* Employ ethical decision-making models, such as the "ethics checklist" or "ethical decision tree," to guide your moral reasoning process systematically. These models provide structured steps for ethical analysis.

   - *Consider Ethical Questions:* Ask yourself a series of ethical questions relevant to the situation, such as "What are my duties in this context?" or "What principles are at stake?" This systematic approach can help clarify your ethical stance.

Chapter 6

The Influence of Culture and Society on Moral Decision-making

The Impact of Culture on Moral Beliefs And Values

Culture profoundly shapes our moral beliefs and values. It serves as the crucible in which our ethical principles are forged and refined. This chapter explores how culture exerts its influence on our moral compass, examining the cultural determinants of ethics, the role of cultural relativism, and strategies for navigating cultural diversity in the moral landscape.

Cultural Determinants of Ethics

Culture is a powerful determinant of our ethical framework. It imbues us with a set of shared beliefs, norms, and values that guide our moral decision-making. These cultural determinants include:

1. **Upbringing and Socialization:** From a young age, we are socialised into our culture's moral fabric. Our families, communities, and educational systems install in us the fundamental principles that define right and wrong.

2. **Religion and Spirituality:** Religious and spiritual beliefs often play a central role in shaping moral values. These systems provide a

moral code that dictates behaviour and offers a framework for understanding ethical dilemmas.

3. **Laws and Governance:** Legal systems within a culture reflect its moral values. The laws we live under are a manifestation of societal ethics, reflecting what is considered acceptable and punishable.

4. **Social Norms and Customs:** Cultural norms dictate how we interact with others and what behaviour is deemed appropriate or taboo. These norms inform our ethical behaviour in social settings.

5. **Historical and Societal Context:** The history and societal context of a culture influence its moral development. Past events, such as wars or revolutions, can shape collective ethical values and priorities.

Cultural Relativism

Cultural relativism is the idea that ethical standards are culturally determined, and there is no universal moral truth. Instead, what is considered morally right or wrong varies from one culture to another. While cultural relativism acknowledges the diversity of moral beliefs worldwide, it raises important questions:

  The Art of Moral Decision Making

Is there a place for moral universals amidst cultural diversity? Are there certain ethical principles that transcend cultural boundaries? The debate between cultural relativism and moral universals is ongoing, and it underscores the complexity of the interplay between culture and ethics.

Navigating Cultural Diversity in Morality

In an increasingly interconnected world, individuals often encounter cultural diversity in moral beliefs and values. Navigating these differences requires sensitivity and open-mindedness. Here are strategies for doing so:

1. **Cultural Empathy:** Cultivate empathy by seeking to understand the cultural context that shapes others' moral beliefs. Put yourself in their shoes to appreciate the reasons behind their ethical perspectives.

2. **Cross-Cultural Dialogue:** Engage in open and respectful dialogue with individuals from different cultural backgrounds. Conversations can foster mutual understanding and reveal shared ethical concerns.

3. **Ethical Relativism vs. Universalism:** Consider the balance between ethical relativism and

universalism. While respecting cultural diversity, reflect on whether there are ethical principles that transcend cultures and are worthy of universal recognition.

4. **Ethical Decision-Making Models:** Utilize ethical decision-making models that account for cultural factors. These models can help individuals navigate complex moral dilemmas in culturally diverse contexts.

5. **Ethical Pragmatism:** Embrace ethical pragmatism when faced with cultural diversity. Sometimes, finding common ground and practical solutions that respect cultural values is more productive than rigidly adhering to one's own ethical perspective.

6. **Ethical Codes and Guidelines:** Organizations and institutions often provide ethical codes and guidelines that navigate cultural diversity. Familiarise yourself with these resources and use them as a framework for ethical decision-making.

Impact of Globalization

Globalization has intensified the interplay between culture and morality. As cultures interact and intermingle, individuals are exposed to a multitude of ethical perspectives. This exposure can lead to both cultural enrichment and ethical conflicts. In the globalised world, individuals must:

1. **Adaptability:** Cultivate adaptability in navigating diverse cultural environments. An open and flexible mindset can help individuals respond effectively to various ethical challenges.

2. **Intercultural Communication:** Develop strong intercultural communication skills to bridge gaps in understanding. Effective communication can promote ethical harmony in culturally diverse settings.

3. **Ethical Global Citizenship:** Embrace the concept of ethical global citizenship. As responsible global citizens, individuals have a duty to respect cultural diversity while upholding universal ethical principles.

Culture serves as a profound influencer of our moral beliefs and values. It shapes our ethical framework through upbringing, religion, laws, social norms, and historical context. Cultural relativism underscores the diversity of moral perspectives across cultures, while the debate on moral universals highlights the search for ethical principles that transcend cultural boundaries.

Navigating cultural diversity in morality requires empathy, dialogue, and adaptability. As the world becomes increasingly interconnected, individuals must cultivate the skills and mindset to engage ethically with diverse cultural perspectives. In doing so, they contribute to a more inclusive and harmonious global moral landscape, where cultural diversity is respected, and universal ethical principles are upheld.

The impact of culture on moral beliefs and values is an ever-evolving topic, reflecting the dynamic nature of human societies. As cultures continue to interact and influence one another, the ethical tapestry of our global community will inevitably evolve, making the exploration of this relationship an ongoing and vital endeavour.

The Role of Socialization in Shaping Moral Decision-Making

Socialization is a powerful force in molding our moral decision-making. From the moment we enter the world, we are immersed in a web of social influences that guide our ethical compass. This chapter delves into the profound role of socialization in shaping our moral values, exploring the impact of family, peers, education, media, and society at large.

Family and Early Influences

1. **Family Values:** The family is the primary agent of socialization. It is within our families that we first encounter moral values and principles. Parents and caregivers transmit their own ethical beliefs through daily interactions, shaping our initial understanding of right and wrong.

2. **Modelling Behaviour:** Children often model their behaviour after the adults in their lives. Observing how parents and caregivers respond to moral dilemmas sets early examples of ethical decision-making.

3. **Moral Education:** Family conversations and rituals contribute to moral education.

Discussing ethical questions, sharing stories, and engaging in family traditions can install moral values and reinforce ethical behaviour.

Peer Influence

1. **Peer Norms:** As children grow, peer relationships become increasingly influential. Peer groups establish their own norms and codes of conduct, shaping the moral values of their members.

2. **Peer Pressure:** Peer pressure can influence moral decision-making, leading individuals to conform to the moral standards of their peer group, even if those standards conflict with their family's values.

3. **Moral Dilemmas:** Interactions with peers can present moral dilemmas that challenge an individual's ethical beliefs and force them to navigate conflicting values.

Education and Academic Settings

1. **Moral Education Programs:** Schools and educational institutions often implement moral education programs to foster ethical development. These programs teach values such as honesty, empathy, and respect.

2. **Moral Role Models:** Teachers and mentors can serve as moral role models, guiding students in ethical decision-making through their own actions and guidance.

3. **Classroom Discussions:** Ethical discussions in the classroom provide opportunities for students to explore and debate moral issues, enhancing their moral reasoning skills.

Media and Technology

1. **Media Messages:** Mass media, including television, movies, and the internet, shape our moral perceptions. Media messages can reinforce or challenge societal values, influencing moral decision-making.

2. **Exposure to Diverse Perspectives:** Exposure to diverse cultural and ethical perspectives through media can broaden an individual's understanding of morality and encourage empathy.

3. **Media Literacy:** Developing media literacy skills is crucial in critically evaluating the ethical content presented in various forms of media.

Society at Large

1. **Cultural Norms:** Societal norms and values play a significant role in shaping individual moral decisions. Cultural norms define what is considered acceptable or taboo within a society.

2. **Legal Systems:** Legal systems codify societal ethics into laws and regulations, influencing individual behaviour through the threat of punishment and the promise of justice.

3. **Social Movements:** Social movements and advocacy groups work to change societal norms and values, impacting moral decision-making on a larger scale.

Challenges in Socialization

While socialization is a potent force in shaping moral decision-making, it also presents challenges:

1. **Cultural and Generational Differences:** Conflicts can arise when individuals from different cultural backgrounds or generations hold disparate moral values. Negotiating these differences requires empathy and understanding.

2. **Ethical Dilemmas:** Socialization can create moral dilemmas when an individual's family values conflict with societal norms or peer group expectations.

3. **Critical Thinking:** The pressure to conform to social norms or peer group standards can sometimes stifle critical thinking and independent moral reasoning.

Strategies for Navigating Socialization in Moral Decision-Making

Navigating the influence of socialization on moral decision-making requires self-awareness and ethical resilience. Here are strategies to consider:

1. **Self-Reflection:** Engage in self-reflection to recognize the influence of socialization on your moral values and decisions. Understand the sources of your ethical beliefs.

2. **Open-Mindedness:** Cultivate an open-minded approach to morality. Be willing to consider and evaluate different ethical perspectives, even if they challenge your own.

3. **Ethical Autonomy:** Strive for ethical autonomy by developing the ability to make moral

decisions independently, free from undue external pressure.

4. **Ethical Dialogue:** Engage in ethical dialogue with others, including family, peers, and mentors. Discussing moral dilemmas and perspectives can sharpen your ethical reasoning.

5. **Media Literacy:** Develop media literacy skills to critically evaluate the ethical content presented in various forms of media. Be conscious of media's potential influence on your moral perceptions.

6. **Cultural Competence:** When navigating diverse cultural norms and values, seek to understand and respect different perspectives. Be culturally competent in your interactions.

7. **Moral Principles:** Identify and uphold your core moral principles, even in the face of social pressure. Know when to stand by your ethical convictions.

Socialization is a potent force in shaping our moral decision-making. It begins in the family, continues through peer relationships and education, and extends into the broader influence of media, culture, and society. While socialization plays a pivotal role in ethical development, it also presents challenges and conflicts.

Navigating the complex interplay between socialization and morality requires self-awareness, critical thinking, and ethical resilience. By understanding the sources of our moral values, engaging in ethical dialogue, and upholding our core ethical principles, we can make more informed and ethically sound decisions in the face of social influences.

Ultimately, our ability to navigate the intricate relationship between socialization and moral decision-making empowers us to live in harmony with our deeply held values while engaging constructively with the diverse ethical landscape of our interconnected world.

The Impact of Cultural Differences on Moral Decision-Making

Cultural differences exert a profound influence on our moral decision-making processes. As individuals from diverse cultural backgrounds encounter one another in an increasingly interconnected world, understanding how these differences shape ethical judgments becomes essential. This chapter delves into the ways cultural variations impact moral beliefs, values, and actions.

Cultural Relativism

Cultural relativism posits that ethical standards are culturally determined, and there is no universal moral truth. Instead, moral values are shaped by the cultural context in which individuals are socialised. This perspective highlights the importance of understanding cultural differences in moral decision-making.

Cultural Dimensions

Cultural dimensions, as proposed by social psychologist Geert Hofstede, provide a framework for understanding how cultural variations influence moral decision-making. These dimensions include:

     The Art of Moral Decision Making

1. **Individualism vs. Collectivism:**

   - *Individualistic Cultures:* Emphasize personal autonomy, individual rights, and self-expression in moral decision-making.

   - *Collectivistic Cultures:* Prioritize group harmony, interdependence, and communal values in ethical judgments.

2. **Power Distance:**

   - *High Power Distance Cultures:* Tend to accept hierarchical authority and status differences in moral decisions.

   - *Low Power Distance Cultures:* Favor egalitarianism and equality in ethical reasoning.

3. **Uncertainty Avoidance:**

   - *High Uncertainty Avoidance Cultures:* Prefer clear rules and structure in moral dilemmas.

   - *Low Uncertainty Avoidance Cultures:* Are more tolerant of ambiguity and uncertainty in ethical decision-making.

4. **Masculinity vs. Femininity:**

   - *Masculine Cultures:* Emphasize competition, achievement, and assertiveness in ethical judgments.

- *Feminine Cultures:* Prioritize cooperation, nurturing, and relationship-building in moral decision-making.

5. **Long-Term vs. Short-Term Orientation:**

   - *Long-Term Orientation Cultures:* Focus on future goals, perseverance, and tradition in ethical reasoning.

   - *Short-Term Orientation Cultures:* Emphasize immediate gratification, adaptability, and pragmatic solutions in moral decisions.

Impact on Moral Decision-Making

1. **Moral Values and Priorities:** Cultural differences shape moral values and priorities. For example, cultures that prioritize collectivism may place a higher value on family and community welfare in moral decisions.

2. **Ethical Dilemmas:** Cultural variations can result in different interpretations of ethical dilemmas. What is considered an ethical conflict in one culture may be perceived differently in another.

3. **Decision-Making Processes:** Cultural differences influence the decision-making process. Some cultures may engage in more

The Art of Moral Decision Making

communal decision-making, while others emphasize individual autonomy.

4. **Moral Judgment and Consequences:** Cultural values impact moral judgments and the perceived consequences of actions. An action deemed morally acceptable in one culture may be seen as morally reprehensible in another.

Navigating Cultural Differences in Moral Decision-Making

Effectively navigating cultural differences in moral decision-making requires sensitivity, empathy, and cross-cultural communication skills. Here are strategies to consider:

1. **Cultural Empathy:** Develop cultural empathy by seeking to understand the cultural context that shapes others' moral beliefs and values. Be open to perspectives that differ from your own.

2. **Cross-Cultural Dialogue:** Engage in open and respectful cross-cultural dialogue. Conversations with individuals from diverse backgrounds can foster mutual understanding.

3. **Cultural Awareness:** Cultivate cultural awareness by studying and familiarising

yourself with the cultural dimensions and values of different societies.

4. **Ethical Relativism vs. Universalism:** Reflect on the balance between ethical relativism and universalism. While respecting cultural diversity, consider whether there are ethical principles that transcend cultures.

5. **Ethical Autonomy:** Strive for ethical autonomy by making informed ethical decisions based on your values and principles while respecting cultural differences.

6. **Ethical Decision-Making Models:** Utilize ethical decision-making models that consider cultural factors. These models can guide ethical analysis in cross-cultural contexts.

7. **Ethical Competence:** Develop ethical competence in navigating cultural differences. Be prepared to adapt your approach to accommodate diverse perspectives.

8. **Ethical Pragmatism:** Embrace ethical pragmatism when faced with cultural diversity. Seek common ground and practical solutions that respect cultural values.

Cultural differences play a pivotal role in shaping our moral decision-making processes. Cultural relativism reminds us that ethical values are context-dependent and that understanding diverse perspectives is essential. The cultural dimensions framework provides insights into how specific cultural values influence moral beliefs and actions.

Navigating cultural differences in moral decision-making demands empathy, open-mindedness, and effective cross-cultural communication. As the world becomes increasingly interconnected, individuals who can engage constructively with diverse cultural perspectives contribute to a more inclusive and harmonious global moral landscape, where cultural diversity is respected, and universal ethical principles are upheld.

The impact of cultural differences on moral decision-making underscores the need for continued exploration and dialogue in this ever-evolving field. As cultures continue to interact and influence one another, our understanding of the intricate relationship between culture and morality will undoubtedly deepen and expand, enriching our collective ethical tapestry.

Chapter 7

The Psychology of Moral Dilemmas

The Nature of Moral Dilemmas

Moral dilemmas are the crucibles in which our ethical principles are tested. These complex situations require individuals to navigate conflicting moral values, leading to challenging decisions with profound consequences. This chapter delves into the nature of moral dilemmas, exploring their characteristics, classification, and the factors that contribute to their complexity.

Characteristics of Moral Dilemmas

1. **Conflict of Values:** Moral dilemmas arise when individuals are confronted with conflicting values or ethical principles. They must choose between competing moral imperatives.

2. **No Clear Right Answer:** Unlike straightforward ethical decisions, moral dilemmas lack a clear "right" answer. Individuals must make choices amid uncertainty and ambiguity.

3. **Ethical Consequences:** Moral dilemmas involve ethical consequences that may impact the well-being of individuals, groups, or society as a whole.

4. **Emotional Weight:** Moral dilemmas often evoke strong emotions, such as guilt, fear, or anxiety, due to the difficult choices they present.

5. **Ethical Principles at Odds:** Dilemmas frequently pit fundamental ethical principles against one another, such as the conflict between the principle of autonomy and the principle of beneficence in medical ethics.

Classification of Moral Dilemmas

Moral dilemmas can be classified into several categories based on the nature of the conflict they present:

1. **Ethical vs. Pragmatic Dilemmas:** Ethical dilemmas involve conflicts between moral values or principles. Pragmatic dilemmas involve conflicts between practical considerations, such as financial constraints or resource allocation.

2. **Moral vs. Non-Moral Dilemmas:** Moral dilemmas involve questions of right and wrong. Non-moral dilemmas involve decisions that do not have inherent ethical implications, such as choosing between two equally enjoyable leisure activities.

3. **Personal vs. Professional Dilemmas:** Personal dilemmas occur in an individual's personal life, while professional dilemmas arise within the context of their occupation or role.

4. **Intrapersonal vs. Interpersonal Dilemmas:** Intrapersonal dilemmas involve conflicts within an individual's own values or beliefs. Interpersonal dilemmas involve conflicts between individuals or groups.

Factors Contributing to Complexity

Several factors contribute to the complexity of moral dilemmas:

1. **Ethical Pluralism:** The existence of multiple ethical frameworks and moral principles can lead to conflicting judgments about what is morally right or wrong.

2. **Contextual Variables:** The context in which a moral dilemma unfolds can significantly impact the decision-making process. Factors such as cultural norms, legal constraints, and personal relationships influence choices.

3. **Emotional Influence:** Emotions, including empathy, fear, anger, and guilt, can sway ethical

decisions, making it challenging to maintain objectivity.

4. **Moral Uncertainty:** Moral dilemmas often involve uncertainty about the consequences of different choices, making it difficult to predict the outcome of one's decision.

5. **Moral Reasoning Styles:** Individuals may employ different styles of moral reasoning, such as deontological (rule-based) or consequentialist (outcome-based) reasoning, leading to divergent ethical judgments.

Resolving Moral Dilemmas

While moral dilemmas lack a straightforward solution, individuals can employ various strategies to navigate them:

1. **Ethical Frameworks:** Utilize ethical frameworks, such as deontology, utilitarianism, or virtue ethics, to analyze the dilemma systematically.

2. **Consultation:** Seek input and advice from trusted individuals or experts who can provide diverse perspectives and guidance.

3. **Reflective Reasoning:** Engage in reflective moral reasoning by considering the long-term consequences and ethical implications of each choice.

4. **Consider Consequences:** Assess the potential consequences of different choices, weighing the benefits and harms to individuals or groups affected.

5. **Ethical Principles:** Uphold core ethical principles, such as honesty, fairness, and justice, as guiding principles in the decision-making process.

Moral dilemmas are the crucibles of ethical decision-making, characterized by conflicts of values, ambiguity, and emotional weight. They defy simple solutions, challenging individuals to grapple with complex ethical choices.

Classified into various categories and influenced by factors such as ethical pluralism, contextual variables, and emotional influence, moral dilemmas present intricate challenges. However, by employing ethical frameworks, seeking consultation, engaging in reflective reasoning, and considering consequences, individuals can navigate these dilemmas with greater ethical clarity and integrity. While moral dilemmas test our ethical resolve, they also offer opportunities for growth and moral development. Through the thoughtful consideration of conflicting values and principles, individuals can refine their ethical judgment and deepen their understanding of the complex nature of moral decision-making.

The Impact of Moral Dilemmas on Moral Decision-Making

Moral dilemmas are crucibles of ethical decision-making. They force individuals to confront conflicting values and principles, challenging their moral resolve. This chapter delves into how moral dilemmas impact moral decision-making, exploring the cognitive processes, emotional responses, and ethical growth that arise in the face of these ethical conundrums.

Cognitive Processes in Moral Dilemmas

Moral dilemmas engage various cognitive processes that influence decision-making:

1. **Moral Reasoning:** Individuals engage in moral reasoning, applying ethical principles and frameworks to evaluate the options before them.

2. **Perspective-Taking:** Cognitive empathy involves taking the perspective of others involved in the dilemma, considering their feelings, thoughts, and values.

3. **Ethical Deliberation:** Ethical deliberation entails reflecting on the consequences, duties,

and virtues associated with each choice, seeking an ethically sound resolution.

4. **Conflict Resolution:** Individuals engage in internal conflict resolution, attempting to reconcile conflicting values or principles.

Emotional Responses to Moral Dilemmas

Moral dilemmas evoke a range of emotional responses that influence decision-making:

1. **Guilt and Shame:** Facing moral conflict can evoke guilt or shame, particularly when individuals believe their decision may harm others or violate their own ethical principles.

2. **Empathy:** Empathetic responses may arise as individuals consider the impact of their choices on others, leading to compassionate decision-making.

3. **Anger and Frustration:** Frustration and anger may emerge when individuals perceive the dilemma as unjust or when their ethical principles clash with external pressures.

4. **Anxiety and Stress:** The uncertainty and weight of moral dilemmas can lead to anxiety and stress, affecting the clarity of decision-making.

Impact on Ethical Growth

Moral dilemmas have a profound impact on ethical growth and development:

1. **Ethical Awareness:** Dilemmas heighten ethical awareness, prompting individuals to examine their values and beliefs more closely.

2. **Ethical Decision-Making Skills:** Navigating moral dilemmas enhances ethical decision-making skills, fostering the ability to make more informed and principled choices.

3. **Moral Development:** Moral dilemmas contribute to moral development, enabling individuals to refine their ethical principles and judgment.

4. **Resilience:** Confronting moral dilemmas builds ethical resilience, allowing individuals to face future ethical challenges with greater confidence.

Factors Influencing Decision-Making in Moral Dilemmas

Several factors influence how individuals make decisions in moral dilemmas:

1. **Cultural Values:** Cultural values and norms shape the ethical frameworks individuals apply to dilemmas, influencing their choices.

2. **Personal Values:** Personal values play a central role in decision-making, as individuals seek to align their choices with their deeply held beliefs.

3. **Emotional Regulation:** The ability to regulate emotions can impact decision-making, as heightened emotions may cloud ethical judgment.

4. **Ethical Principles:** The prominence of ethical principles, such as autonomy, justice, or beneficence, can vary, leading to different ethical resolutions.

5. **Social and Peer Pressure:** External influences, including peer pressure or societal expectations, can sway decisions in moral dilemmas.

6. **Consequences and Risk Assessment:** The assessment of potential consequences and risks associated with each choice can guide decision-making.

Navigating Moral Dilemmas Effectively

Effectively navigating moral dilemmas requires a thoughtful approach:

1. **Ethical Reflection:** Engage in ethical reflection to clarify personal values and principles before confronting dilemmas.

2. **Emotional Awareness:** Cultivate emotional awareness to recognize and manage emotional responses during decision-making.

3. **Ethical Frameworks:** Utilize ethical frameworks, such as deontology, utilitarianism, or virtue ethics, to guide moral reasoning.

4. **Ethical Consultation:** Seek ethical consultation or engage in dialogue with trusted individuals to gain diverse perspectives.

5. **Ethical Autonomy:** Strive for ethical autonomy by making principled decisions aligned with personal values.

Moral dilemmas are pivotal moments in ethical decision-making, engaging cognitive processes, evoking emotional responses, and fostering ethical growth. They challenge individuals to navigate conflicting values and principles, leading to complex choices with profound consequences.

Understanding the cognitive and emotional dynamics of moral dilemmas allows individuals to approach them more effectively. By reflecting on personal values, applying ethical frameworks, and seeking consultation when needed, individuals can make more informed and principled decisions in the face of these ethical conundrums.

Ultimately, moral dilemmas are not just tests of ethical resolve; they are opportunities for ethical growth and development. Confronting these dilemmas enables individuals to refine their values, enhance their ethical decision-making skills, and contribute to a more ethically aware and responsible society.

Strategies For Resolving Moral Dilemmas

Resolving moral dilemmas is a complex endeavor that demands careful consideration and ethical insight. Individuals facing such dilemmas often grapple with conflicting values and principles, seeking a path that aligns with their moral compass. This chapter explores various strategies for effectively resolving moral dilemmas, offering guidance on how to navigate these intricate ethical challenges.

1. **Ethical Frameworks:** Utilize established ethical frameworks, such as deontology, utilitarianism, virtue ethics, or the ethics of care, to guide your moral reasoning. These frameworks provide structured approaches for evaluating dilemmas.

2. **Consequential Analysis:** Assess the potential consequences of each course of action in the dilemma. Consider short-term and long-term outcomes, both positive and negative, for all stakeholders involved.

3. **Principle-Based Decision-Making:** Identify and prioritize the ethical principles that are

most relevant to the dilemma. Consider principles such as autonomy, beneficence, non-maleficence, and justice in your analysis.

4. **Consult Trusted Advisors:** Seek advice and guidance from trusted individuals, mentors, or ethical experts who can offer diverse perspectives and help you navigate the complexities of the dilemma.

5. **Reflective Reasoning:** Engage in reflective moral reasoning by contemplating the moral dimensions of the dilemma. Reflect on how your values and principles apply to the situation and whether they lead to a particular course of action.

6. **Ethical Deliberation:** Deliberate on the ethical implications of each choice. Consider the duties, obligations, and virtues associated with different courses of action.

7. **Ethical Dialogue:** Engage in open and respectful ethical dialogue with others involved in the dilemma. Discussing the ethical aspects of the situation can lead to a deeper understanding and potential resolutions.

8. **Empathy and Perspective-Taking:** Put yourself in the shoes of those affected by your decision. Consider their feelings, thoughts, and values, fostering empathy and a broader perspective on the dilemma.

9. **Hypothetical Testing:** Imagine hypothetical scenarios that explore the potential consequences of your choices. This thought experiment can help you anticipate the ramifications of different decisions.

10. **Seek Common Ground:** Look for areas of common ground or compromise that respect the values and interests of all parties involved. Strive for solutions that maximize overall well-being and justice.

11. **Ethical Autonomy:** Cultivate ethical autonomy by making decisions based on your own values and principles, rather than succumbing to external pressures or conformity.

12. **Ethical Codes and Guidelines:** In professional settings, refer to ethical codes, guidelines, or regulations that apply to your field. These frameworks can offer valuable guidance in resolving dilemmas.

13. **Consider Consequences:** Analyze the consequences of your decisions not only for immediate stakeholders but also for society at large. Consider the broader ethical implications of your choices.

14. **Evaluate Long-Term Impact:** Assess how your decisions may affect the long-term well-being of individuals and communities. Strive for solutions that promote sustained ethical outcomes.

15. **Ethical Education and Training:** Invest in ongoing ethical education and training to enhance your ethical reasoning skills. Attend workshops, seminars, or courses focused on ethics and moral decision-making.

16. **Role Models and Case Studies:** Study real-life ethical case studies and examine how individuals or organizations have navigated similar dilemmas. Role models and case studies can provide valuable insights.

17. **Ethical Autopsy:** After making a decision, conduct an "ethical autopsy" to evaluate the outcome and reflect on whether it aligns with

your values and principles. Learn from the experience to inform future decisions.

18. **Ethical Checks and Balances:** Establish ethical checks and balances within organizations or groups to ensure that decisions align with ethical standards. Encourage open discussions about ethical concerns.

19. **Seek Legal Counsel:** In situations where legal aspects are involved, consider seeking legal counsel to ensure that your decisions comply with relevant laws and regulations.

20. **Review and Adapt:** Continuously review and adapt your decision-making strategies in response to evolving ethical challenges and changing circumstances.

Resolving moral dilemmas is a complex and demanding task, but it is essential for maintaining ethical integrity and promoting ethical growth. By employing these strategies and approaches, individuals can navigate the intricate ethical landscapes of dilemmas more effectively. While dilemmas test our ethical resolve, they also offer opportunities for moral development and a deeper understanding of the complexities of moral decision-making.

Chapter 8

The Ethics of Moral Decision-Making

The Nature Of Ethical Decision-Making

Ethical decision-making is a fundamental aspect of human life. It involves the process of evaluating choices and actions to determine what is morally right or wrong. This chapter explores the nature of ethical decision-making, delving into the components, factors, and models that shape our ethical judgments and actions.

Components of Ethical Decision-Making

Ethical decision-making consists of several key components:

1. **Moral Agents:** Moral agents are individuals or entities responsible for making ethical decisions. They possess the capacity to reason about moral principles and take actions based on their judgments.

2. **Ethical Issues:** Ethical issues are situations or dilemmas that raise questions about what is morally right or wrong. These issues form the basis for ethical decision-making.

3. **Ethical Principles:** Ethical principles are fundamental values and guidelines that inform

moral judgments. Common principles include honesty, fairness, justice, autonomy, and beneficence.

4. **Moral Reasoning:** Moral reasoning involves the process of evaluating ethical issues and dilemmas by applying ethical principles and frameworks.

5. **Moral Judgment:** Moral judgment is the outcome of moral reasoning, resulting in a decision or determination of what is morally appropriate or acceptable.

6. **Ethical Action:** Ethical action involves implementing the chosen course of action that aligns with one's moral judgment.

Factors Influencing Ethical Decision-Making

Ethical decision-making is influenced by various factors:

1. **Personal Values:** Personal values, shaped by upbringing, culture, and life experiences, play a significant role in ethical decision-making.

2. **Ethical Frameworks:** Individuals may employ ethical frameworks, such as deontology,

                    The Art of Moral Decision Making

utilitarianism, virtue ethics, or relativism, to guide their moral reasoning.

3. **Social and Cultural Norms:** Societal and cultural norms influence ethical judgments by shaping what is considered morally acceptable or unacceptable.

4. **Emotional Responses:** Emotions, such as empathy, guilt, anger, or fear, can impact moral judgments and actions.

5. **Context and Situational Factors:** The specific context and situational factors surrounding an ethical issue can influence decision-making. Factors may include time pressure, peer pressure, or available resources.

6. **Consequences and Outcomes:** The anticipated consequences of actions and the potential impact on individuals or society are crucial considerations in ethical decision-making.

Models of Ethical Decision-Making

Several models offer structured approaches to ethical decision-making:

1. **The Utilitarian Model:** The utilitarian model assesses ethical choices based on their potential

to maximize overall happiness or minimise harm. Decisions aim to produce the greatest net benefit.

2. **The Deontological Model:** Deontology emphasizes adherence to ethical principles and duties regardless of the consequences. Actions are judged as intrinsically right or wrong.

3. **The Virtue Ethics Model:** Virtue ethics focuses on the development of virtuous character traits. Decisions are guided by virtues such as honesty, courage, and compassion.

4. **The Rights-Based Model:** Rights-based ethics centers on respecting individuals' rights and autonomy. Decisions prioritize protecting and upholding fundamental rights.

5. **The Care Ethics Model:** Care ethics emphasizes empathetic and compassionate responses to ethical dilemmas. Decisions prioritize relationships and care for others.

6. **The Casuistry Model:** Casuistry involves analyzing ethical cases by comparing them to paradigm cases with well-established moral judgments. Decisions are made by analogy.

The Process of Ethical Decision-Making

Ethical decision-making often follows a systematic process:

1. **Recognize the Ethical Issue:** Identify the ethical dilemma or issue at hand, acknowledging that it raises moral questions.

2. **Gather Information:** Collect relevant information about the situation, including facts, context, and stakeholders involved.

3. **Identify Ethical Principles:** Determine the ethical principles and values that are applicable to the situation.

4. **Engage in Moral Reasoning:** Analyze the ethical issue by applying ethical frameworks and principles. Consider potential courses of action and their consequences.

5. **Make a Moral Judgment:** Reach a moral judgment by selecting the course of action that aligns with ethical principles and values.

6. **Implement Ethical Action:** Take the chosen ethical action based on the moral judgment.

7. **Reflect and Learn:** Afterward, reflect on the decision and its consequences, learning from the experience for future ethical challenges.

Ethical decision-making is a multifaceted process driven by moral agents, ethical issues, principles, reasoning, judgment, and action. It is influenced by personal values, cultural norms, emotional responses, and the specific context of ethical dilemmas.

Various ethical frameworks and models offer structured approaches to decision-making, each with its own emphasis on consequences, principles, virtues, rights, care, or casuistry. The process of ethical decision-making involves recognizing ethical issues, gathering information, identifying principles, engaging in moral reasoning, making judgments, implementing actions, and reflecting on the outcomes.

Understanding the nature of ethical decision-making is essential for individuals and organizations seeking to navigate complex ethical landscapes with integrity and responsibility. Ethical decision-making not only shapes individual character but also contributes to the ethical fabric of societies and institutions, fostering trust, fairness, and justice in human interactions.

The Role Of Ethical Principles In Moral Decision-Making

Ethical principles are the foundation upon which moral decision-making is built. These principles serve as guiding lights, providing individuals with a framework to evaluate actions and choices in light of what is considered morally right or wrong. This chapter delves into the critical role of ethical principles in moral decision-making, exploring their significance, diversity, and application.

The Significance of Ethical Principles

Ethical principles are significant for several reasons:

1. **Providing Guidance:** Ethical principles offer clear and consistent guidance for individuals when facing moral dilemmas or ethical decisions. They help answer the question, "What should I do?"

2. **Promoting Moral Consistency:** Ethical principles encourage moral consistency by providing a set of moral standards against which actions and decisions can be assessed.

3. **Upholding Ethical Values:** Ethical principles are the means by which individuals can uphold and express their ethical values and beliefs.

4. **Fostering Accountability:** Ethical principles hold individuals accountable for their actions, as they provide a basis for evaluating the moral rightness or wrongness of behaviours.

5. **Resolving Ethical Dilemmas:** Ethical principles serve as tools for resolving ethical dilemmas by helping individuals weigh conflicting values and make informed choices.

Diversity of Ethical Principles

Ethical principles encompass a diverse range of values and approaches. Some of the most prominent ethical principles include:

1. **Autonomy:** Autonomy emphasizes the right of individuals to make decisions about their own lives and bodies. It respects personal freedom and self-determination.

2. **Beneficence:** Beneficence promotes actions that benefit others and contribute to their well-being. It encourages altruism and the prevention of harm.

3. **Non-Maleficence:** Non-maleficence dictates the obligation to do no harm. It guides individuals to avoid actions that could cause harm or suffering to others.

4. **Justice:** Justice emphasizes fairness and the equitable distribution of resources and opportunities. It calls for the just treatment of individuals and groups.

5. **Veracity:** Veracity underscores the importance of truthfulness and honesty in interactions. It discourages deception and falsehood.

6. **Fidelity:** Fidelity stresses the importance of keeping promises, honoring commitments, and maintaining trust in relationships.

7. **Utility:** Utility, rooted in utilitarianism, advocates actions that maximize overall happiness or minimize suffering, prioritizing the greatest good for the greatest number.

8. **Virtues:** Virtue ethics focuses on cultivating virtuous character traits such as honesty, courage, compassion, and integrity. It emphasizes the importance of moral virtues in decision-making.

Application of Ethical Principles

Ethical principles are applied in various contexts and domains, including:

1. **Medical Ethics:** In healthcare, principles like autonomy, beneficence, and non-maleficence guide medical professionals in making ethical decisions about patient care and treatment.

2. **Business Ethics:** In the business world, principles of honesty, fairness, and justice inform ethical practices related to corporate governance, employee treatment, and customer relations.

3. **Environmental Ethics:** Environmental ethics draw on principles of stewardship, sustainability, and responsibility to guide decisions regarding the preservation and protection of the natural world.

4. **Legal Ethics:** Legal ethics are based on principles of justice, confidentiality, and the duty of zealous representation. They govern the conduct of lawyers and judges.

5. **Research Ethics:** In research, ethical principles guide the treatment of human and animal

     The Art of Moral Decision Making

subjects, ensuring their rights and welfare are respected.

6. **Everyday Decision-Making:** In everyday life, ethical principles help individuals make moral decisions about honesty, integrity, and fairness in their interactions with others.

Balancing Ethical Principles

Ethical decision-making often requires individuals to balance competing ethical principles. For example, a medical professional may need to weigh a patient's autonomy (the right to make choices) against beneficence (the duty to do what is best for the patient) when making treatment decisions. The process of balancing ethical principles is not always straightforward and may involve trade-offs. Individuals must consider the specific context and consequences of their decisions to determine the most ethically justifiable course of action.

Ethical Principles and Cultural Variations

Cultural variations can influence the interpretation and application of ethical principles. What is considered morally right or wrong may vary across cultures and societies. For example, the importance placed on individual autonomy may differ between cultures with collectivist and individualist values.

Understanding these cultural variations is essential for navigating diverse ethical landscapes and respecting different perspectives on ethical principles.

Ethical principles are the cornerstone of moral decision-making, providing guidance, consistency, and accountability. They encompass a wide range of values and approaches, allowing individuals to address diverse ethical dilemmas in various contexts. Applying ethical principles requires careful consideration of competing values and the recognition that ethical decision-making

The Impact of Ethical Considerations on Moral Decision-Making

Ethical considerations play a pivotal role in shaping the moral landscape of decision-making. These considerations encompass a wide range of principles, values, and ethical frameworks that guide individuals in discerning what is morally right or wrong. This chapter explores the profound impact of ethical considerations on the process of moral decision-making, emphasizing their significance, influence, and application.

The Significance of Ethical Considerations

Ethical considerations hold significant importance in decision-making for several key reasons:

1. **Guiding Moral Judgments:** Ethical considerations provide individuals with a moral compass, helping them navigate complex dilemmas and make informed moral judgments.

2. **Fostering Accountability:** Ethical considerations hold individuals accountable for their actions, encouraging them to act in accordance with ethical principles and values.

3. **Promoting Ethical Integrity:** Ethical considerations contribute to the development of ethical integrity, shaping character and reinforcing adherence to moral standards.

4. **Enhancing Ethical Clarity:** Ethical considerations bring clarity to ambiguous situations by offering a framework for evaluating choices and behaviours.

5. **Resolving Ethical Dilemmas:** In the face of ethical dilemmas, ethical considerations help individuals weigh conflicting values and principles, facilitating resolution.

Influence of Ethical Considerations

Ethical considerations wield significant influence over the decision-making process:

1. **Ethical Principles:** Ethical principles, such as autonomy, beneficence, justice, and veracity, guide decision-making by providing a foundation for evaluating actions.

2. **Moral Reasoning:** Ethical considerations drive moral reasoning, prompting individuals to apply ethical principles and frameworks to assess situations.

     The Art of Moral Decision Making

3. **Emotional Responses:** Ethical considerations can evoke emotions such as empathy, guilt, or moral outrage, influencing the emotional component of decision-making.

4. **Cultural and Societal Norms:** Cultural and societal norms are often shaped by ethical considerations, impacting what is considered morally acceptable or unacceptable.

5. **Personal Values:** Personal values, deeply influenced by ethical considerations, inform individual moral judgments and actions.

6. **Contextual Factors:** Ethical considerations interact with contextual factors, such as the specific circumstances of a decision, to shape its ethical dimension.

Application of Ethical Considerations

Ethical considerations find application in various domains and contexts:

1. **Healthcare:** In healthcare, ethical considerations inform decisions about patient care, treatment options, informed consent, and end-of-life care.

2. **Business:** Ethical considerations guide business practices related to corporate

responsibility, employee treatment, consumer relations, and environmental sustainability.

3. **Law and Justice:** In the legal field, ethical considerations underpin principles of justice, fairness, and the duty of lawyers and judges to uphold the law.

4. **Research and Academia:** Ethical considerations govern research involving human subjects, animal welfare, and the integrity of academic scholarship.

5. **Environmental Ethics:** Environmental ethics rely on ethical considerations to address issues related to ecological sustainability, conservation, and environmental protection.

6. **Social and Interpersonal Relations:** Ethical considerations shape how individuals interact with one another in everyday life, influencing honesty, integrity, and trustworthiness.

Balancing Ethical Considerations

Ethical decision-making often entails balancing multiple ethical considerations, which can sometimes conflict. For instance, in healthcare, the principles of autonomy and beneficence may clash when a patient's choice contradicts what is believed to be in their best interest.

The process of balancing ethical considerations requires careful assessment, weighing the relative importance of each consideration in the given context, and striving for ethically justifiable outcomes.

Cultural Variations in Ethical Considerations

Cultural variations can significantly impact the interpretation and application of ethical considerations. What is considered morally right or wrong may differ across cultures and societies due to variations in values, norms, and ethical frameworks.

Understanding these cultural variations is essential for fostering cross-cultural respect and dialogue and recognizing the diversity of ethical perspectives.

Ethical Considerations in Ethical Decision-Making Models

Ethical decision-making models, such as utilitarianism, deontology, virtue ethics, and care ethics, incorporate ethical considerations into their frameworks. These models offer structured approaches to decision-making by emphasizing specific ethical principles and values.

Ethical considerations are foundational to moral decision-making, guiding individuals in discerning what is morally right or wrong. They play a pivotal role in shaping moral judgments, fostering ethical integrity, and promoting accountability.

Influence is exerted through ethical principles, moral reasoning, emotional responses, cultural norms, personal values, and contextual factors. Ethical considerations find application across diverse domains, including healthcare, business, law, research, and interpersonal relations.

Balancing ethical considerations and recognizing cultural variations in ethical perspectives are essential aspects of ethical decision-making. Ultimately, ethical considerations enrich the moral landscape of decision-making, contributing to the development of ethical character and the cultivation of ethical societies where values such as justice, honesty, and compassion are upheld.